God's Way and Knowing the King

Maintain a Personal Relationship with The True and Living God!

AUDREY L. DICKEY, PH.D.

Kingdom Advance Publishing
P. O. Box 48288
Los Angeles, California 90048
877.333.5075

robertandaudreydickeyministries.org

Printed in the United States of America

ISBN: 978-0-9997611-7-5

Library of Congress Control Number: 2018905670
Kingdom Advance Publishing, Los Angeles, CA

Christian Life / Relationship / Spiritual Growth

DEDICATION

I dedicate this book to You, JESUS, my Lord, my God, of whose family I am. I worship and honor You as King of Glory, the King of kings and the Lord of lords! You are my closest, dearest and most faithful Friend. I trust You explicitly with my very life and soul for eternity.

I love You and look forward to Your move of unprecedented Glory!

CONTENTS

Introduction   ix

Chapter

1.   The Name that is Above Every Name   11

2.   The Person Jesus   55

3.   The Commission Sent from Heaven   95

4.   The Gift, His Anointing Abides in
     You   141

5.   His Love, a More Excellent Way   163

6.   His Kingdom, Kingship and Royal
     Power   185

7.   The King of kings and You   233

Appendix A:
     A Prayer for Salvation and the Infilling
     of Holy Spirit   289

Appendix B:
     What is Salvation?   293

Appendix C:
  Supernatural Prayer Language   299

Notes   321

INTRODUCTION

The very foundation and reason for this material is to shed some light on a mystery many feel they cannot solve. The mystery of having a personal intimate relationship with God Himself is because of their past or what they have been taught about God.

Know this, He is not so far off in the heavens, too big to notice you, too mean or angry to care. The mystery of Who He really is, how accessible He is and how much He really cares is revealed in this resource.

Time is short! Now is the hour to know *WHO* He is and *WHAT* He is about. He is a *person*; a *Spiritual Being* and we were made in His image after His likeness. We too are spiritual beings but we live in a body and we have a soul (a mind, will and emotions), John 4:24; Genesis 1:26; and I Thessalonians 5:23. His name, character, purpose for being sent to earth from heaven and what He brought from heaven no longer has to be a mystery.

His power, His forgiveness, and His love are beyond the world we live in. Find out why God, the King of kings and Lord of lords, the Creator of all things would desire to have a personal relationship with you!

Be set free to bask in the Presence of Almighty God; your God, your Father and your Friend! It is never too late to build and embrace a personal relationship with the Great I AM!

Furthermore, you will learn many things you did not know about Him. Audrey shares from her heart about the Friend she was introduced to at a time in her adult life when she was experiencing great pain from watching her family ripped apart. At the time, not realizing she was in a spiritual battle.

She shares from a thirty-year journey that brought her to a place where *no person could ever convince her God does not exist.*

God loves you and He wants to be close to you. You are a part of His family and He does not take that lightly. As a matter of fact, He is so serious about it He was willing to die to save His family from a doomed eternity to everlasting life with Him where there is peace and fulfillment.

Jesus has a specific plan and purpose for each and every one that has chosen Him to be a part of their present and future, Jeremiah 29:11.

Let us explore through these pages together and find out exactly *who* He is, *what* He is about and *how* we fit into His life and He into ours!

Chapter 1

The Name that is Above Every Name

What is in a name? A name can describe what you are about. It can describe your character. Your name identifies you and could be connected to your fame (people remember your name, which represents you, and is based on what you have done).

In the Bible, names are important. During biblical times a name was an expression of the nature, character and destiny of an individual. It could also reflect physical attributes such as in Esau's case who had red hair, so he was given a name that was the color red. Simon's name was changed from Simon to Peter which meant "rock" to reflect his call and destiny. A name is a revelation of a person, it can describe what they are about.

When God gives a name, it will come with an anointing to help the person accomplish the purpose associated with their calling.

God's name is a revelation and/or expression of His character, purpose and His nature as well. You will receive understanding and insight to who He is and what He is like and how He relates to you.

The more revelation we have about Him the greater our faith in Him will be because we will know His character and thereby come to know Him, I John 2:3-6. If we know Him, we know we can trust in the names that represent Him. We also please Him with our faith when we are willing to, with His grace, follow His instructions.

Yeshua HaMashiach is Hebrew for Jesus the Messiah, the Anointed One, Who is known to most as "Jesus Christ." He is our Lord and Savior; our High Priest and the King of Glory to those who know and love Him. We will explore other names, titles and attributes further on.

His Personal name is Jesus or Yeshua, which signifies Savior or Salvation. The name given to the angel Gabriel to give to Mary (Miriam in Hebrew), Jesus/Yeshua's Mother, Luke 1:26-31. This was the name given before He was conceived in the womb of Mary by Holy Spirit.

He was also named by an angel who was sent to Joseph, a descendant of David, in a supernatural dream in respect to Mary and the Child. Joseph was promised in marriage to Mary but "before they came together, she was found to be pregnant [through the power] of Holy Spirit," Matthew 1:18-20.

Matthew 1:21-25 Further Explains,

She will bear a Son, and you shall call His name Jesus [the Greek form of the

Hebrew Joshua, which means Savior], for He will save His people from their sins [that is, prevent them from failing and missing the true end and scope of life, which is God]. All this took place that it might be fulfilled which the Lord had spoken through the prophet, Behold, the virgin shall become pregnant and give birth to a Son, and they shall call His name Emmanuel--which, when translated, means, God with us. Then Joseph, being aroused from his sleep, did as the angel of the Lord had commanded him: he took [her to his side as] his wife. But he had no union with her as her husband until she had borne *her firstborn* Son; and he called His name Jesus.

All Authority was Given to the Name that is Above Every Name

Jesus declared all authority was His before He gave the Great Commission.

It says in Matthew 28:18-20,

Jesus approached and, breaking the silence, said to them, **All authority (all power of rule) in heaven and on earth has been given to Me.** Go then and make disciples of all the nations, baptizing them into the name of the Father and of the Son and of the Holy Spirit, Teaching them to observe everything that I have commanded you, and behold, I am with you all the days (perpetually, uniformly, and on every occasion), to the [very] close *and* consummation of the age. *Amen (so let it be).* (Emphasis added.)

In addition, in John 14:13-14, Jesus tells us He will grant whatever we ask in His name. In that, He presents all that He is, so His Father in Heaven may be glorified through the Son.

Yet, even having been given all authority in heaven and on earth, He surpassed Moses to become truly the most humble person whoever walked the face of the earth. "And after He had appeared in human form, He abased and humbled Himself [still further] and carried His obedience to the extreme of death even the death of the cross! Phil. 2:8; Gal. 3:13.

Because of His Stance He is Exalted, Philippians 2:9,

Therefore, [because He stooped so low] God has highly exalted Him and has freely *bestowed on Him the name that is above every name.* (Emphasis added.)

"That in (at) the name of Jesus every knee should (must) bow, in heaven and on earth and under the earth, And every tongue [frankly and openly] confess *and* acknowledge that Jesus Christ is Lord, to the glory of God the Father," Philippians 2:10-11. He has great compassion, yet He never compromised His position or His Word. This is one of the reasons we can have total confidence in His name and in the Word of God.

Through His Name We Can Better Understand His Identity

To know Him better one must understand His identity. **Jesus Christ is not His first and last name** (His given and family name). When we say, Jesus Christ, we are saying, Jesus the Messiah. Jesus is the English translation from the Greek which is pronounced I-e-sous. Later around the fifteenth century new sounds were added to the language and the "I" was changed to the letter "J." In addition, His Hebrew name Yeshua in English would be Joshua. Names may change their spelling when you translate them from language to language.

In Hebrew Yeshua means Salvation or God Saves. Why was this name chosen for Him? Because

His purpose was to save His people from their sins through Salvation. Throughout the Old Testament (Torah, Tanakh, Old Covenant) when reference is made to Salvation it is referring to Yeshua or Jesus, Isaiah 12:2 and in Psalm 62:2 it says, "He only is my Rock and my Salvation, my Defense *and* my Fortress, I shall not be greatly moved."

As mentioned above, **Christ is not His last name. Christ means the "Anointed One."** The Greek word Christos comes from the Hebrew word Mashiach (Christos – Christ - the Anointed One, Isaiah 61:1). The Hebrew word Mashiach or Messiah (Christ) is Jesus' official title. Jesus was anointed to minister on this earth as an Apostle, Prophet, Preacher, Teacher and so forth. He baptized His followers with Holy Spirit, John 1:33. He also brought forth through His atonement on the cross Salvation for all those in the world who will receive this gift.

How God Identified Himself

The Holy Scriptures in the Old Testament (Old Covenant) and in the New Testament (New Covenant) make it very clear and confirm we worship "One God" in accordance with and by the way He identifies Himself.

Exodus 3:14 States in the Old Testament Regarding I AM,

And God said to Moses, I AM WHO I AM *and* WHAT I AM, *and* I WILL BE WHAT I WILL BE; and He said, You shall say this to the Israelites: I AM has sent me to you!

Isaiah 41:4 States in the Old Testament Regarding I AM,

Who has prepared and done this, calling forth *and* guiding the destinies of the generations [of the nations] from the beginning? I, the Lord--the first [existing before history began] and with the last [an ever-present, unchanging God]--I am He.

John 8:58 States in the New Testament Regarding I AM,

Jesus replied, I assure you, most solemnly I tell you, before Abraham was born, I AM.

Luke 22:67-70 Says in the New Testament Regarding I AM,

If You are the Christ (the Messiah), tell us. But He said to them, If I tell you, you will not believe (trust in, cleave to, and rely on what I say), And if I question you, you will not answer. But hereafter (from this time on), the Son of Man shall be seated at the right hand of the power of God. And they all said, You are the Son of God, then? And He said to them, It is just as you say; I AM.

John 14:9 in the New Testament says,

Jesus replied, Have I been with all of you for so long a time, and do you not recognize *and* know Me yet, Philip? Anyone who has seen Me has seen the Father. How can you say then, Show us the Father?

When Moses asked for God's name, so he could go "to the Israelites and say to them, The God of your fathers has sent me to you... And God said to Moses, I AM WHO I AM *and* WHAT I AM, *and* I WILL BE WHAT I WILL BE; and He said, You shall say this to the Israelites: I AM has sent me to you! God said also to Moses, This shall you say to the Israelites: The Lord, the God of your fathers, of Abraham, of Isaac, and of Jacob, has sent me to you! *This is My name forever, and by this name I am to be remembered to all generations,"* Exodus 3:13-15; Psalm 135:13.

I AM, is everyone and everything to all. He says, "there is no other God besides Him," Isaiah 45:5-6. He can take care of anything you encounter in life. He can be that special someone to you that is missing in your life, such as a parent, a brother, a friend and so forth. He said He would never leave you. He created all, did all, He is the Great I AM. He promised the descendants of Jacob a just reward. He speaks righteousness and truth. He declares things that are right, and He is the One Who will be with you always! Isaiah 45:18-25.

In John 8:58 above, Jesus was saying He is the Self-Existent LORD, the God Who always IS. He identified Himself as Yahweh the Covenant God of Israel. As stated in Philippians 2:10 NKJV, "that at the name of Jesus every knee should bow, of those in heaven, and of those on earth, and of those under the earth." Why? Because He is the Messiah, Almighty God!

Therefore, whatever you need, God is "I AM." Our God has no limitations, He is generous with His love, peace, provision, prosperity, joy, strength, faithfulness and all that is needed to make us whole. All that is needed to ensure the abundant life He laid His life down to give to us is in Him, is in His Name.

We are not to take His Name lightly. He is asking us to Honor His Name because it represents Who He Is. When we pray "Hallowed be Your name," (Matthew 6:9) we are declaring "May Your Name be honored! We understand and agree His Name can be trusted as holy (set apart and special only to be used for righteousness and good).

Therefore, "I will exalt you, my God the King; I will praise your name for ever and ever. Every day I will praise you and extol your name for ever and ever," Psalm 145-1-2 NIV.

In the book of John Jesus refers to Himself as "I AM" seven times.

He said,

"I **am** the Light of the world," John 8:12.
"I **am** the Good Shepherd," John 10:11.
"I **am** the Door," John 10:9.
"I **am** the Vine," John 15:5.
"I **am** the Bread of Life," John 6:35.
"I **am** the Way, the Truth and the Life," John 14:6
"I **am** the Resurrection and the Life," John 11:25
(Emphasis added.)

So, as we worship, know we worship One God, The True and Living God! His Word tells us why and how we are to worship Him, Revelation 1:8.

God is a Spirit, John 4:23-26,

A time will come, however, indeed it is already here, when the true (genuine) worshipers will worship the Father in spirit and in truth (reality); for the Father is seeking just such people as these as His worshipers. *God is a Spirit (a spiritual Being) and those who worship Him must worship Him in spirit and in truth (reality).* (Emphasis added.)

The woman said to Him, I know that Messiah is coming, He Who is called the Christ (the Anointed One); and when He arrives, He will tell us everything we need to know *and* make it clear to us. Jesus said to her, I Who now speak with you am He.

God *is* Spirit
(a spiritual Being)
John 4:24 NKJV, AMP

I AM

SPIRIT

God the Father   God the Son   God Holy Spirit

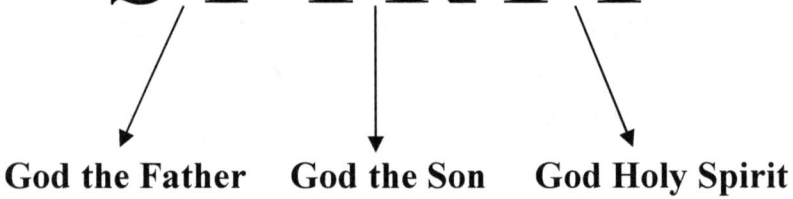

One God:
Three different manifestations
Three different Persons

Genesis 1:26; Hebrews 1:2 AMP

The Great "I AM"

Exodus 3:14; John 8:58 AMP

"Be still, and know that I *am* God;
I will be exalted among the nations,
I will be exalted in the earth!"

Psalm 46:10 NKJV

Where He Places His Name, His Presence Follows

God will have a dwelling place where He will place His Name and His presence will dwell among you. In 2 Sam. 7:13-14 He speaks of David's offspring building Him a house, **"He shall build a house for My Name [and My Presence],** and I will establish the throne of his kingdom forever. I will be his Father, and he shall be My son.

A Place for God's Name is a Place for His Presence, Deut. 12:5,

> But you shall seek the place which the Lord your God shall choose out of all your tribes to put His Name and make His dwelling place, and there shall you come.

After the Lord appeared to Abram, he built an altar where the Lord had appeared and spoke to him. Wherever He places His name even if it is an altar built from stones as Abram did in Genesis 12:7, God's presence will show up. In this case it was built after God showed this was a place His presence visited or will visit again.

"The 'Name' of God is equivalent to His gracious presence in passages such as this one. The place where God puts His Name is the place where the Lord Himself, chooses to dwell. When it stands for God's presence at the sanctuary, 'Name' is capitalized." (Amplified Bible Deuteronomy 12 Footnote.)

When God directs you to a place of worship He will direct you somewhere where His name and all that goes with it is welcomed. You will be able to dwell in His presence (His glory) and be fulfilled by His Spirit.

His Holy Spirit should have liberty to do all that is necessary to set the captives free, to heal the wounded and brokenhearted and to equip and train the Believers for the work of ministering toward building up His Kingdom, Isa. 61:1; Luke 4:18; Eph. 4:12.

The Believers will also walk in their dominion which was given at the beginning when God set mankind into time, which was stolen and has been restored by our Lord and Savior Who paid a dear price to recapture it back from the enemy for us.

We Can Worship and Praise God by Speaking Descriptive Names that Glorify Him during a Praise Break!

The Lord desires that we Honor His Name! When we do we are worshipping Him and can receive from Him. As we praise His name we are worshipping Him. For an example, Yahweh Rophe in Hebrews says, I AM your Healer, Acts 3:16. As you declare and believe what He has declared about Himself you can receive it for yourself (take hold of it for yourself or someone else's healing you are believing for).

In Reference to Praising His Name, Isaiah 25:1 says,

> O LORD, You are my God; I will exalt You, *I will praise Your name,* for You have done wonderful things, even purposes planned of old [and fulfilled] in faithfulness and truth. (Emphasis added.)

YHVH (Yod-Heh-Vav-Heh in Hebrew), I AM He Who Is; Barukh Hashem, Bless the Name. *Yeshua HaMashiach is Jesus the Messiah; Jesus the Christ; the Anointed One!* He says, I Am Love; I Am Holy; I Am Truth; I Am Spirit; I Am the Door. *"I Am the Way, the Truth and the Life. No one comes to the Father except through Me;"* I AM the Great I AM! Father of Peace, I worship You Father, I worship You Jesus (Yeshua), I worship You Holy Spirit. Jesus is my Hope of Glory, I honor and adore You. You are the Resurrection and the Life. *You are all powerful and all power is in Your hands.* You are my Joy; I worship You Lord. I will bless the Lord forever. You are a sure Foundation. You are my Light and Salvation; my Rock; I find my hope, strength and healing in You. You are Wonderful, Counselor, Mighty God, Everlasting Father and Prince of Peace. My peace is in You because You are the Prince of Peace and You chose to leave Your Peace for me. You are the True Vine; You are Omnipresent (everywhere); Omnipotent (all powerful); and Omniscient (all knowing). When I come boldly to the throne of Grace Your door is always open as I enter Your gates with thanksgiving and Your courts with praise. You are my Precious Father, my Precious Lord, and my Precious Holy Spirit. *Before the Beginning You were and there is no End in You; You always were and You always will be.* You are the King of kings, the Lord of lords and the Champion of champions. You are the King of Glory. You are all powerful and all power is in Your hands. You are my Friend, You are the Light of the world, You are worthy of all praise watching over Your Word to perform it and you are no respecter of persons. You are Faithful and Holy (set apart and special). I welcome Your Presence into my life each and every day. *You never change, You are the same Yesterday, Today and Forever.* Your Spirit is my Helper, my Advocate, my Teacher, my Comforter, my Strengthener, my Deliverer, my Vindicator and my Father of Mercy. You reveal mysteries to me because You are the Revealer. You are my Joy and a miracle working God. You created and beautified the Heavens and the earth by Your

Holy Spirit for my enjoyment. You are upholding all things by the Power of Your Word. Great protection is in You. You give me peaceful sleep and rest for my soul. I have great comfort in You. You are the Lamb of God, the Holy One of Israel, the Last Adam, and the Last Sacrifice. **You are worthy of all Honor and all Praise, that is why I praise Your Holy, Holy, Holy Name!** Psalm 145:1-3.

Joshua a Type and Shadow of Jesus

Joshua was appointed and anointed to lead the Israelites out of the wilderness into the Promise Land. He and Caleb were the only two people over the age of twenty from the original group who left Egypt with Moses that actually went into their promise, Joshua 6. It was forty years from the time the twelve spies spied out the land and ten of them fell into doubt and fear of taking the land, Exo. 13:26-33. Joshua and Caleb were the only two spies that believed they could take the land with God's help and because of their faith they went in with the sons and daughters of the ones that died in the wilderness because of their unbelief.

Joshua's name is an English translation that also means salvation. He led the Israelites out of the wilderness into God's promise, overcame their enemies and restored their inheritance. They entered into God's "Shalom," the wholeness and peace He had for them. They became Overcomers.

Yeshua/Jesus is our Overcomer, John 16:33 NKJV declares, "These things, I have spoken to you, that in Me you may have peace. In the world you will have tribulation; but be of good cheer, I have overcome the world."

Jesus is also leading His church out of the wilderness (their circumstances in life) into "The Blessing" as He reintroduces to His church the structure of government (Eph. 4:11) He placed on the earth in the Early Church. This structure will advance and keep His Kingdom in a position of authority and abundance (prosperity), John 10:10; Psalms 35:27. Thus they will come into their inheritance. (See *God's Way and Finances* for more details regarding the inheritance, the blessing, prosperity and the financial life God really has for those who are a part of His Kingdom.)

Therefore, Joshua's assignment was a type and shadow of what the Messiah will accomplish for His people in the End-Times.

What is the Meaning of Shalom?

Shalom is to have true peace, a peace that passes all understanding and prevents your heart from being troubled. This peace can only be obtained when you are *whole*. Therefore, it implies wholeness – *Shalom.*

Shalom is a Hebrew word when translated into English means *peace.*

Shalom is spoken primarily from one Jewish person to another as a form of greeting. It asks the other, is anything broken about you? Do you have all your goods? Are you at peace? The objective is to find out if the person is "whole." Is there anything missing or broken in your life? An often-used reply is simply, "H' col b'seder - The whole is in order." In other words, the reply is, all is well with me, thank you for asking. Usually this is preceded by Barukh HaShem which is bless the Name!

So, shalom centers around the meaning, "wholeness" and when we are whole we have peace. This peace comes from listening to God and accepting His ways and path for our lives. We find His purpose and will for all of mankind in His Word. Yet He is truly the only One who knows our true purpose as an individual for being on the face of the earth. When we seek Him and the answer is revealed we will have the beginning of the peace He left for us to enjoy.

The Word of God is the Holy Bible which is comprised of the Old and New Testaments. They are also referred to as the Old and New Covenants. In Hebrew the Holy Bible is called the Tanakh. For those that read the New Covenant, in Hebrew it is called B'rit Hadashah. The New Covenant was prophesied in Jeremiah 31:31-33 and delivered by Jesus as shown in Luke 22:20; Matthew 26:26-29 and spoken about in various scriptures including Hebrews 8: 10, 12.

In both covenants "Every Scripture is God-breathed (given by His inspiration) and profitable for instruction, for reproof *and* conviction of sin, for correction of error *and* discipline in obedience, [and] for training in righteousness (in holy living, in conformity to God's will in thought, purpose, and action)," 2 Timothy 3:16. It goes on to say in verse 17 NIV "so that the servant of God may be thoroughly equipped for every good work."

Therefore, as we study and learn of God and choose to follow His ways and not those of men (mankind), we will obtain a peace that goes beyond understanding, Phil. 4:6-7; Col. 3:2.

John 14:27 in Reference to Peace tells us,

Peace I leave with you; My [own] peace I now give *and* bequeath to you. Not as the world gives do I give to you. Do not let your hearts be troubled, neither let them be afraid. [Stop allowing yourselves to be agitated and disturbed; and do not permit yourselves to be fearful and intimidated and cowardly and unsettled.]

After all, Jesus did not lay His life down to give us "religion" but to give us a "relationship" with Father God. This was made possible through

Jesus, so we could be whole again in Father God's eyes as we were before the fall, Genesis 3.

Because of the blood Jesus shed and was used as the ultimate sacrifice, now when the Father sees us, those that belong to Him, He sees the blood, Romans 5:9; I John 1:7. Therefore, our sins are forgiven and forgotten by God as soon as we ask for forgiveness and repent (change our minds and go in the direction of righteousness).

Therefore, the peace the Messiah brought is Shalom. Peace was re-established through reconciliation between God and His creation of mankind both male and female, Gen. 1:26. With the New Covenant Jesus brought the people that belong to God back in alignment with Father God. And as stated above, this brought an inner peace that comes from being in a state of wholeness.

The shalom that offers wholeness includes: completeness, soundness, welfare, peace, health and prosperity. There is nothing missing and nothing broken concerning you. Therefore, salvation brings you into a state of wholeness and well-being for the whole entire person, spirit, soul and body.

What is Salvation and How is it Connected to God's Name?

God so greatly loved the world He gave His one and only Son, that whoever believes in Him shall not perish but have eternal life, John 3:16. Because of what Jesus (Yeshua) did on the cross, a way was made for people (Jew and Gentile) to be reconciled back to Father God through Salvation.

This brought forth the "Believer," which is the One New Man, Eph. 2:14-16. "And there is salvation in *and* through no one else, *for there is no other name under heaven given among men by and in which we must be saved,"* Acts 4:12, the Amplified Bible.

In John 3:14-17 Jesus explains,

And just as Moses lifted up the serpent in the desert [on a pole], so must [so it is necessary that] the Son of Man be lifted up [on the cross], In order that everyone who believes in Him [who cleaves to Him, trusts Him, and relies on Him] *may not perish, but* have eternal life *and* [actually] live forever! For God so greatly loved *and* dearly prized the world that He [even] gave up His only begotten (unique) Son, so that whoever believes in (trusts in, clings to, relies on) Him shall not perish (come to destruction, be lost) but have eternal (everlasting) life. For God did not send the Son into the world in order to judge (reject, to condemn, to pass sentence on) the world, but that the world might find salvation *and* be made safe *and* sound through Him.

When you receive Yeshua HaMashiach, (Jesus the Christ, the Messiah, the Anointed One) you are saved. "For it is by free grace (God's unmerited favor) that you are saved (delivered from judgment *and* made partakers of Christ's salvation) through [your] faith. And this [salvation] is not of yourselves [of your own doing, it came not through your own striving], but it is the gift of God," Eph. 2:8.

The word "saved" is the English word for the Greek word "Sozo" which was used to define the Hebrew word "Shalom." "To be saved is defined as: to deliver or protect – heal, preserve, save, do well, be (make) whole," (Strong's Concordance).

A personal relationship with God is included. The Holy Spirit is with you, inside of you and will communicate with your spirit (heart). You are also entitled to good health, preservation, protection, provision, prosperity, favor, peace, good relationships, purpose, safety, deliverance, authority, soundness, spiritual gifts, strength, mercy, guidance, angelic help, increase, completeness and more! In other words, wholeness (Shalom).

Furthermore, the English word **"save"** is used in the New Testament to define the Hebrew word **"Shalom."** Another term used to describe "save" is **Born-again.** Jesus said, "unless one is born again, he cannot see the kingdom of God," John 3:1-6; I Peter 1:3.

The name Yeshua (Jesus) means Savior or Salvation. Salvation makes you whole as you grow in Messiah, Matt. 1:21. *Therefore, Yeshua restores "Shalom"* making you whole - nothing broken and nothing missing. He is the Pioneer of your Salvation, Heb. 2:10.

Jesus is also referred to as the Prince of Peace (Sar Shalom) and "Peace comes to you because you are whole!" Hebrews 13:20-21 NKJV says, "Now may the God of peace who brought up our Lord Jesus from the dead, that great Shepherd of the sheep, through the blood of the everlasting covenant, make you complete in every good work to do His will, working in you what is well pleasing in His sight, through Jesus Christ, to whom *be* glory forever and ever. Amen."

To be saved is to have Salvation (Yeshua). Everything you will ever need is found in salvation. *The most important thing about receiving salvation is in Christ you become a new creation; salvation comes with the New Covenant and salvation includes eternal life,* 2 Cor. 5:17; Jeremiah

31:31-33; Matthew 26:26-29; Luke 22:20; Romans 2:28-29; Galatians 2:16 and Galatians 3:7-14; 26-29; John 3:16, 36.

Salvation prevents anyone from perishing for their sin for eternity in outer darkness. Instead of death they will receive eternal life, John 3:36. In addition, while still on earth the Believer receives "The Blessing" which encompasses all the blessings from the Lord in the Kingdom of God.

Because we accepted the Father's sacrifice, Jesus/Yeshua, the Father *adopted us* into His Family (the Family of God, the One New Man).

Romans 8:15 says,

> For [the Spirit which] you have now received [is] not a spirit of slavery to put you once more in bondage to fear, but you have received the Spirit of adoption [the Spirit producing sonship] in [the bliss of] which we cry, Abba (Father)! Father!

The word adoption basically means a person is brought into the Family of God even though they were previously without any covenant with Him. Like all of us who are born-again (John 3:1-3) we were sinners and separated from God, but God in His mercy and grace redeemed us, purchased us and brought us into His presence. In His presence once again, this time through the blood of His only beloved Son, Jesus.

Once saved we are adopted by God, Who chose and received us as His own. What an honor, for Almighty God to choose us and then pour His love on each and every one of us. As Christian Believers in Christ Messiah, the Anointed One.

We are now eternally part of His family. His Spirit dwells in our spirit man and communes with us. Because of the adoption we become heirs of God and joint heirs with His Son, Jesus the Christ (Yeshua HaMashiach), Romans 8:17.

So how does one receive their salvation? Romans 10:9-10 NKJV, "that if you confess with your mouth the Lord Jesus and believe in your heart that God has raised Him from the dead, you will be saved. For with the heart one believes unto righteousness, and with the mouth confession is made unto salvation." (See Appendix A, *A Prayer for Salvation* along with Appendix B, *What is Salvation?*)

His Names, Titles and Attributes Describe His Character

Jesus (Yeshua) is the One name that is above every name. As our Savior He is our High Priest, The Good Shepherd, Bridegroom and Eldest Brother. He is the Head of His family as we are His body, children, bride, joint heirs and sheep. As King

He is our Lord, Master, Commander-in-Chief, Chief Apostle, and Bishop. As Adonai – Lord, a Self-revealing God that wants to relate to you and over see your affairs.

The Lord is declaring Who He is when He says, *"I AM."* For example, *I AM Love* (I John 4:16); *I AM* Holy (I Peter 1:16); *I AM* the Way, the Truth and the Life (John 14:6); *I AM* Spirit (John 4:24); *I AM* the Door (John 10:9); *I AM* the Light of the world (John 8:12); *I AM* the Great I AM (Exodus 3:14)! The name of the Lord is always blessed.

As Jehovah, the LORD, is an expression of Himself as a God of righteousness, holiness, love and redemption. Some additional declarations are: The Holy One, the True One, *"He who has the key of David,* He who opens and no one shuts, and shuts and no one opens" (Rev. 3:7 NKJV), the name of the Lord is a Strong Tower.

Other random names and attributes that help to describe Him: Redeemer; The Holy One of Israel; Rock of Salvation; Lamb of God; Bread of Life; Son of David; Healer; Son of God; The Last Adam; The True Vine; Faithful and True; King of the Ages; Eternal Life; The Author and the Finisher of our faith; Holy Lord of Glory; Light of the World; The Lion of Judah; Our Passover Lamb; Comforter; Teacher; Strengthener; Deliverer; Omniscient; Omnipotent; Omnipresent; King of kings and Lord of lords; my Hope of Glory; The Resurrection and the Life; the Great Shepherd of the sheep; The Word of God; A Miracle working God and Amen (the Beginning and the End) only to name a few of the precious names, titles or attributes that are used in referring to our Endearing Friend (John 15:14) and Personal Savior.

Hebrew Names that Describe Him – Barukh HaShem (Bless the Name)

It is important to know His Name because when you believe whatever He has revealed Himself to be, He will be that to you. His Name is an expression of what He is willing to be to you.

Isaiah 50:10 Explains,

Who is among you who [reverently] fears the Lord, who obeys the voice of His Servant, yet who walks in darkness *and* deep trouble and has no shining splendor [in his heart]? *Let him rely on, trust in, and be confident in the name of the Lord,* and let him lean upon *and* be supported by his God. (Emphasis added.)

Gain faith by knowing Him through His Name. Trusting God's Name is choosing to trust God. Believing what He says about Himself is believing in Him!

I AM - I AM HE WHO IS. I AM, the Great I AM, the Self-Existent One. The Most High God, the Name of the One True God, Who is always present. Also, He reveals Himself, His character and nature by adding other words to His name.

I AM also translates to **YHVH (Yod-Heh-Vav-Heh)**. YHVH in Hebrew is Y'.h.vah or Y'ho.vah and in English Y'hvah or Yahweh and some pronounce it Jehovah in English as well.

Keep in mind when using these names if the person does not believe the name represents the God of Abraham, Isaac and Jacob then they are not speaking about the same God as you. I AM is the God of Israel, Whom He is in covenant with.

Yahweh – I AM; Unchangeable; Intimate God

Yeshua HaMashiach - Jesus the Messiah; Jesus the Christ

EL – Mighty; Strong; Prominent; Strength to accomplish anything

El Shaddai (Shadday) – All Sufficient One. You are Dai – enough

Elohim – God our Sovereign, Mighty Creator; Creative Power

El Gibor – Mighty God

Eloheinu – Our God

Elyon – God Most High

El Olam – God Everlasting

Sar Shalom - Prince of Peace

Yahweh Shalom - I Am your Peace (wholeness); Lord of Sabbath

Yahweh Elohei-Ysrael – I AM the Personal God of Israel

Yahweh Elohay – I AM the Lord your God

Yahweh M'Kaddesh – I AM your Sanctifier

Yahweh Rophe – I AM your Healer; your Health

Yahweh Jireh – I AM your Provider

Yahweh Tsabaoth – I AM the Lord of Hosts

Yahweh Rohi – I AM your Shepherd

Yahweh Tsidkenu – I AM your Righteousness

Yahweh Nissi – I AM your Banner of Victory; Banner aka miracle

Yahweh Shammah – I AM God your Abiding Presence; God is There

Yahweh Makkeh – I AM the Lord Who molds you

Yahweh Gmolah – I AM the Lord Who Rewards

Yahweh Shaphat – I AM the God of Justice

Names, Titles, Attributes with Scriptures
My God Is:

Love - I John 4:16
Spirit - John 4:24
The Holy One - Ps 16:10
All Powerful - Romans 13:1-2; Jer. 32:17, 27
A forgiving God - Mark 11:25; Mt. 6:14
Omnipresent (everywhere/ever present) Ps 139:1-13
Omnipotent (all powerful) - Jeremiah 32:17, 27
Omniscient (all knowing) - I John 3:20
Guarantee of Eternal Life - Eph. 1:13-14
The Great "I AM" - Exo.3:14; John 8:58
The Alpha and Omega, The Beginning and The End –
Rev. 1:8
Unchangeable -Nu. 23:19
A Miracle Working God - Gal. 3:5
The Creator of the World - John 1:3
The Word - John 1:1
God Almighty [El-Shaddai] - Ex 6:3
Yahweh - Exodus 6:3
Jehovah - Exodus 6:3; Ps. 83:18
A Covenant Making God - Heb.10:16
The Everlasting Father – Isaiah 9:6
Faithful and True - Rev. 19:11
Father of Mercies and God of All Comfort - 2 Cor. 1:3
A God Who Raises the Dead - 2 Cor. 1:9
The Author and Pioneer of Salvation - Heb. 2:10
A Quickening Spirit - I Cor. 15:45
Our Heavenly Father - Mt. 6:9
Our Maker – Isaiah 54:5
Jesus my Savior - Matthew 1:21
The Justifier of the One Who Has Faith in Jesus – Ro. 3:26
Meeting needs according to His riches in glory - Phil. 4:19
Giving me the Peace that surpasses understanding - Phil. 4:7
Jesus the Nazarene, the King of the Jews - John 19:19

I Am the Door; who enters through Me will be saved – John 10:9

I Am the Door for the sheep - John 10:7

The Way, the Truth, and the Life - John 14:6

The Prince of Peace; my Peace – Isa. 9:6; Eph. 2:14; John 14:27

The Lord of lords and the King of kings - Rev. 17:14

The Lamb of God - Rev. 5:6

The Bread of Life - John 6:48-58

The Bright and Morning Star - Rev. 22:16

The Light of the World - John 8:12

Emmanuel – Isa. 7:14 and Mt. 1:23

Wonderful, Counselor - Isa 9:6

That Great Shepherd of the sheep - Heb. 13:20

The Foundation, I Cor. 3:11

The Head of the Church - Eph. 1:22

Justifier - Romans 3:26

The same Yesterday, Today and Forever - Heb. 13:8

He is a Warrior, a Man of war – Exo. 15:3

Our all Sufficiency - 2 Cor. 3:5

Infinite - I King 8:27

Dwelling in me & He shall be My God - 2 Cor. 6:16

Easily Touched - Heb. 4:15

Faithful to Complete the Work He began in me - Phil. 1:6

A Sure Foundation - Isa. 28:16

Upholding All Things by the Word of His Power - Heb. 1:3

Watching over His Word to perform it - Jer. 1:12

A Rewarder of those Who Diligently Seek Him - Heb. 11:6

No Respecter of Persons - Acts 10:34

The Author and the Finisher of my Faith - Heb. 12:2

Greater in me than he that is in the world - I John 4:4

Wisdom and Sanctification – I Cor. 1:30

Righteousness and Redemption - I Cor. 1:30

Never leaving me nor forsaking me - Heb. 13:5

Always leading me in Triumph in Christ - 2 Cor. 2:14

Faithful over His house - Heb. 3:1-6

My Lord and My God - John 20:28

My Resurrection and my Life - John 11:25

Whoever believes in Him shall never [actually] die - John 11:26

My Redeemer - Isa. 48:17

The Truth - John 14:6; John 16:13

My Teacher - Matthew 28:18; John 14:26; John 2:20-27

My Healer, is Worthy of all Praise - Isa 53:5; I Peter 2:24; Ps. 18:3

My Deliverer - Romans 11:26

My Comforter, my Strengthener, my Advocate - John 16:7 AMP

My Faithful High Priest - Heb. 9:11 and 10:21

My Foundation - I Cor. 3:11

The Chief Cornerstone – Eph. 2:20

Saying "Surely I Am Coming Quickly" - Rev. 22:20

Why Most Jewish People Do Not Speak or Write God's Name

I have submitted two reports from two different reliable sources below that will attempt to explain this mystery. Both with two entirely different responses.

According to the Complete Jewish Bible by David H. Stern in Exodus 6:3, God's name is Yud-Heh-Vav-Heh (or as some would spell it, Yod-Hey-Vav-Hey) YHVH, is the name of God which the Jews do not speak because "the third commandment prohibits taking God's name in vain, and the man who used it in a curse was put to death at God's explicit instruction." Because it is Holy the Jews substitute Adonay (Adonai) for the name of God which means my Lord. Also, the English rendering of the Tetragrammaton, YHVH is either Yahweh or Yahveh or Jehovah. So, if one would say, "my Lord, my God" in Hebrew they are saying, Adoni ve. Elohai.

The Following was an Interview with Messianic Rabbi Zev Porat of Messiah of Israel Ministries in Israel who Answered Tough Questions Regarding Our Topic. [1]

Question:

Why do Non-Yeshua Believing Jews Globally Avoid Using the Name of God?

Messianic Rabbi Zev Porat Answers:

"If you do a research, before Jesus was on the cross (on the tree) they always pronounced the name of God. Do a research on the first rabbis and on the first Talmud writers. They all mentioned the name of God. It was only sixty or seventy years after Jesus was on the cross that the rabbis, the religious leaders looked at the Bible and they said oh no, we cannot have the Jewish people say this name because if they say this name they are going to believe in Jesus. They are going to believe in Yeshua.

So, the rabbis said we have to make up some kind of a story in order to scare the people, so they will not pronounce the name of God. The enemy (Satan) knows the Bible and he knows in Romans 10:17

it says, faith comes by hearing and hearing by the Word of God.

He also knows His days are numbered, Rev. 20:1-10. So, he uses the spirit of fear through the rabbis, through religion and through many aspects to scare people. Even making certain scripture passages forbidden to read such as Isaiah 53 and Isaiah 7:14 which clearly show Who the Messiah really is in the Old Testament (Tanakh). The rabbis knew that Jesus was the Messiah.

When they looked at God's name after Jesus was on the cross, after He was on the tree, this is where they understood that when Jews start reading God's name they are going to believe in Jesus."

"Rabbi Zev Porat explains what he means. In Hebrew we have twenty-two letters. The first letter of the alphabet is Aleph. The last letter of the Hebrew alphabet is the letter Tav. So, the rabbis do not mention the name of God because if they read the scriptures after Yeshua was the tree and pronounce His name they will know Jesus was the Messiah.

So, lets tell the story the rabbis tell the Jewish people – His name is too holy so, if you pronounce His name they could die or be sick. This is what happened over the generations after the cross. They knew that in God's name is planted the name Yeshua.

The rabbis did not want the Jews to come to faith. They wanted the Jews out of God's provision and blessing, so they would be out of God's salvation. That was the plan. So, the rabbis are terrified by the name of God and it has nothing to do with God's name being holy. God put His Word for us to read not to be scared (afraid) to read it."

Question:

Why are the Non-Yeshua Believing Jews Afraid of the Name of Jesus?

Rabbi Zev Porat Answers:

"The Jewish leaders are always scared of the name of Jesus. Not because they thought He was the Messiah, they knew He was the Messiah. **They were afraid of losing their power and authority**

over the people. And in the same way when they saw God's name in the Bible the Aleph and Tav.

In Revelation in English it says He is Alpha and Omega but in Hebrew it says He is Aleph and Tav. In ancient Hebrew it is not just letters like it is today. It is also pictures. In the time of Moses and Abraham each picture has a meaning. And the rabbis saw the meaning, but they did not understand it *before the cross,* but they understood the meaning after the cross. (Revelation 22:13 AMP "I am the Alpha and the Omega, the First and the Last (the Before all and the End of all."))

The letter Aleph the first letter is a picture of an Oxen and the last letter a Tav is actually a pictograph of a cross bar. Psalm 22 was written before Jesus was on the cross even king David did not understand what it was because there was no cross at that time. There was no Roman Emperor at that time.

They used the picture Aleph before the cross. After the cross they eliminated the original alphabet and wiped it out of school and their history because it points to Jesus.

The name of God spelled in the Bible YHVH we know in English as Yahweh. When Moses asked God who shall I say sent me? God answered, "I AM THAT I AM" which means YHVH. It says behold the hand (behold the nail) and that is the reason why the rabbis say that you cannot pronounce the name of God.

When Jesus walked on the water (Matthew 14:22-33) and the disciples on the boat were afraid, in English verse 27 NKJV was translated that Jesus said, "Be of good cheer! It is I; do not be afraid." In Hebrew it is translated, "Do not be afraid it is the Great I AM." The Great Yahweh, behold the hand, behold the nail. (Emphasis added with scripture by the author, in the Amplified Bible, in Matthew 14:27 Jesus said, "Take courage! I AM! Stop being afraid! And see John 8:58.)

These are the true reasons why the Jews do not pronounce the name of God. The rabbis (those without Holy Spirit) think that if they embrace Jesus as Messiah they believe they are going to lose their power and lose their authority with the people.

He says, they need to go to the Father through Jesus/Yeshua and be teachers of the Word. But they do not view it that way. So, since they believe they will lose all power and Jesus will gain all power, they think we need to get rid of this Jesus. **They cannot see that this is not a knowledge issue, it is a spiritual issue.**

Some have exalted their words and even the Talmud in some cases above the Word of God, the Holy Scriptures. This is a sin and breaks the first commandment of their law in the Old Testament (Old Covenant) he says.

This is a spiritual issue because the leaders at the time of Jesus among other corrupt spirits had a spirit of tradition, pride and stubbornness. Tradition is a wicked powerful demonic spirit that causes a lot of deception in the world of religion.

Rabbi Zev Porat in closing the interview added: God allowed the Israelites to be blinded in part to allow the Gospel to go to the nations (Gentiles – those without a covenant with God) so they could get salvation. *Now it is time to bring the Gospel back to Jerusalem."*

(Emphasis by the author - Religion and tradition cannot stand in the presence of the anointing which is the power of God. Nor will it be in His tangible Presence which is His Glory. This word extends to dead churches who refuse to welcome Holy Spirit in and prefer to operate in tradition and religion.)

Romans 11:11 says,

So I ask, Have they stumbled so as to fall [to their utter spiritual ruin, irretrievably]? By no means! But through their false step *and* transgression salvation [has come] to the Gentiles, so as to arouse Israel [to see and feel what they forfeited] and so to make them jealous.

"Rabbi Zev Porat tells the Believers to not stop using the name of God because you think you are going to offend the Jewish people. The Word of God says, "But whoever denies *and* disowns Me before men, I also will deny *and* disown him before My Father Who is in heaven," Matt. 10:33. In other words, if you are ashamed of Jesus and His teachings then He will be ashamed of you before His Father and the holy angels, Luke 9:26.

The Rabbi says we need to pronounce the name of God and show them that *YHVH is Jesus (Yeshua).* He says, show the love for the Jewish people and the nations (the lost) with the Truth!"

The Author's Conclusion

Remember it is not wise to follow opinions of men regardless of their status, office or roll; whether they are a rabbi, a pastor, an evangelist, or any other ministry office. If what a person says does not line up with the Word of the Living God, which is our standard, then what they say is not to be taken literally.

We worship a God that cannot lie. Therefore, we are only required to follow "Truth" because that is the only thing that will set you free with liberty, joy, and the wholeness (Shalom) that we all need while we are in this life. The Lord Jesus said, I AM the Truth, John 14:6. So, if we follow Him we will reach our destiny and fulfill our purpose.

Our Messiah Does Not Lie, Numbers 23:19,

God is not a man, that He should tell *or* act a lie, neither the son of man, that He should feel repentance *or* compunction [for what He has promised]. Has He said and shall He not do it? Or has He spoken and shall He not make it good?

Chapter 2
The Person Jesus

Jesus the Messiah is my God, my Father, my Helper and my Friend. A Friend that is closer than any person. He is the Light of the World, the Lamb of God and the Rose of Sharon. He is the Alpha and the Omega, the Pioneer of my salvation, the Bread of Life and the Chief Cornerstone of His church. He is the King of kings and the Lord of lords.

He is Yeshua (Jesus), YHVH (Yahweh), the covenant God of Israel. He is the Lord of the Harvest, the Lord of Glory, the Prince of Peace, Emmanuel God with us, and the Bright and Morning Star! And He shall *return* as the Lion of the Tribe of Judah.

We could go on and on with descriptive names but there are not enough words to describe the magnitude of Who He is and the Greatness He holds. ***Therefore, it is written whatever you need Me to be "I AM."***

Jesus is the Second Person of the Trinity

Father, Son and Holy Spirit are One God, Genesis 1:26 Amplified Bible; One Spirit, John 4:24. Yet three different Persons with three different manifestations! They are known as the Trinity. Father being the Creative Mind (soul); Jesus incarnate (body) and Holy Spirit (spirit/breath).

Proverbs 30:4-5 says,

> Who has ascended into heaven and descended? Who has gathered the wind in His fists? Who has bound the waters in His garment? Who has established all the ends of the earth? What is His name, and what is His Son's name, if you know?

Jesus (Yeshua) was and is the Son of God. Really, He is God manifested in the Second Person of the Trinity and as Christ the Messiah, the Anointed One, He is the Manifestation of the Third Person of the Trinity! He is Spirit and His Spirit has the power and the capacity to be everywhere (Omnipresent) in the same moment.

God made us in His image, Genesis 1:26. Just as He is three in One so is His creation of man, meaning there are three parts to mankind (male and female) as well. They are spirit, soul and body, I Thess. 5:23. Furthermore, we are on the earth and yet we are seated in heavenly places with Christ.

Ephesians 2:6-7 says,

> And He raised us up together with Him and made us sit down together [giving us joint seating with Him] in the heavenly sphere [by virtue of our being] in Christ Jesus (the Messiah, the Anointed One). He did this that He might clearly demonstrate through the ages to come the immeasurable (limitless, surpassing) riches of His free grace (His unmerited favor) in [His] kindness *and* goodness of heart toward us in Christ Jesus.

The Lord is Also the Manifested Incarnate Word of God Who was Given Life by the Spirit of God

In John 1:1 it says, "In the beginning [before all time] was the Word (Christ), and the Word was with God, and the Word was God Himself." However, when the Word came to dwell among men a body was prepared for Jesus to dwell on the earth. Jesus said in verse seven, "...Behold, here I am, coming to do Your will, O God— [to fulfill] what is written of Me in the volume of the Book." The Bible further says in verse ten, "And in accordance with this will [of God], we have been made holy (consecrated and sanctified) through the offering made once for all of the body of Jesus Christ (the Anointed One)," Hebrews 10:5-10.

Therefore, the Spirit of God (Holy Spirit) caused Mary the mother of Jesus to conceive and bring forth a Son and the Word manifested on the earth to fulfill the will of Almighty God. Matthew 1:18 says, "Now the birth of Jesus Christ took place under these circumstances: When His mother Mary had been promised in marriage to Joseph, before they came together, she was found to be pregnant [through the power] of the Holy Spirit."

Also seen in Luke 1:26-38 NKJV which gives a full account of Jesus' conception with the body that was sent from Heaven. An angel told His Mother in verses 32-33 NKJV, "He will be great, and will be called the Son of the Highest; ... And He will reign over the house of Jacob forever, and of His kingdom there will be no end." Verses 34-35 NKJV says, Mary asked, "How can this be, since I do not know a man? And the angel answered and said to her, "The Holy Spirit will come upon you, and the power of the Highest will overshadow you; therefore, also, that Holy One who is to be born will be called the Son of God."

Therefore, the Lord is Word and Spirit. Without the Spirit the Word of God becomes legalistic, creating dry dead religion, endless traditions and customs. The Spirit breathes the very life into the written Word of God. It is the breath that brings the words to life and make them living words from a living God. It is the breath of God that activates the words.

Jesus said in reference to Father God in John 4:23-24, "...God is a Spirit (a spiritual Being) and those who worship *Him* must worship Him in spirit and in truth (reality)."

The Word of God is anointed to change the lives of Born-again, saved individuals (all those Jew or Gentile who have received their salvation). The Bible is an instruction book for God's people. As they seek Him in His Word the Words come alive and gives them instructions, revelation and direction for their lives.

The Spirit of God Gives Life, John 6:63,

It is the Spirit Who gives life [He is the Life-giver]; the flesh conveys no benefit whatever [there is no profit in it]. The words (truths) that I have been speaking to you are spirit and life.

Therefore, truth and spirit are the foundations our relationship with our God is based upon. When we search for truth, the written Word of God is truth and the revelation that Holy Spirit gives us as we study the Word. And as we seek revelation the Holy Spirit is a Revealer, Teacher, Counselor, Helper and so forth who will come and be in close fellowship with us, John 16:7. So, our faith should be based on both truth and the spirit.

Furthermore, the Spirit of God is also called the "Spirit of Truth (the Truth-giving Spirit)." When He comes He will guide us into all the Truth. He will bring whatever message the Father has for us. Holy Spirit will honor *and* glorify Jesus, because He will take of what is His and will reveal it to you, John 16:13-14.

I Am the Way, the Truth, and the Life

The Lord is "the Way" to the Father. He is our salvation which reconciles us back to Father God. Jesus will restore the relationship that was severed after the fall of mankind: male and female, Gen. 3; John 14:6; John 10:7.

The Lord will reveal "the truth" to you when you ask. He will give you the courage to face truth. Truth is valuable and very much needed to bring and maintain peace in our lives. Truth exposes lies and deception that were sent by the father of lies, John 8:44. Truth will open doors and cause favor and God's ways to manifest in our lives. As we choose to believe truth and apply it to our lives it will set us free, John 8:32. As we choose to believe the Truth about the Messiah and Who He is, we will be free, Eph. 4:15. He is a God that cannot lie, Nu. 23:19.

Titus 1:1-2 Explains,

> PAUL, A bond servant of God and an apostle (a special messenger) of Jesus Christ (the Messiah) to stimulate *and* promote the faith of God's chosen ones and to lead them on to accurate discernment *and* recognition of *and* acquaintance with the Truth which belongs to *and* harmonizes with *and* tends to godliness, [Resting] in the hope of eternal life, [life] which the ever truthful God Who cannot deceive promised before the world *or* the ages of time began.

Because of the redemption offered by Christ the Anointed One, we can receive "the Life" that has been offered. A life that never ends because we have eternal life in Him. After death we continue in eternal life that lasts forever. Only He who is Life can give life, John 14:6, John 6:28.

Romans 6:23 says,

> ...the gift of God *is* eternal life in Christ Jesus our Lord.

As we seek Him in His Word and in prayer we will come to know Him. As we receive the written and the spiritual we will go beyond just knowing Him in our minds but *to know Him in our hearts (spirit).* In I John 2:3 it says, "And this is how we may discern [daily, by experience] that we are coming to know Him [to perceive, recognize, understand, and become better acquainted with Him]: if we keep (bear in mind, observe, practice) His teachings (precepts, commandments)" which are basically His instructions, we will come to know the *Living God!*

"Blessed *be* the God and Father of our Lord Jesus Christ, who has blessed us with every *spiritual blessing* in the heavenly *places* in Christ... to the praise of the glory of His grace, by which He made us accepted in the Beloved," Eph. 1:3, 6 NKJV.

Conception and the Eternal Unbreakable Blood Covenant

Mankind was redeemed by the price of blood. The New Covenant in Christ differs from the Old Covenant because the New Covenant is eternal -- *the Lamb of God, the Lord Jesus shed His blood to seal this covenant forever making it the strongest covenant in the earth today.* Because of His sacrifice this covenant also blesses us with every spiritual blessing in the heavenly realm, Ephesians 1:3.

Hebrews 13:20-21 says,

Now may the God of peace [Who is the Author and the Giver of peace], Who brought again from among the dead our Lord Jesus, that great Shepherd of the sheep, by **the blood [that sealed, ratified] the everlasting agreement (covenant, testament),** strengthen (complete, perfect) and make you what you ought to be and equip you with everything good that you may carry out His will; [while He Himself] works in you and accomplishes that which is pleasing in His sight, through Jesus Christ (the Messiah); to Whom be the glory forever and ever (to the ages of the ages) Amen (so be it). (Emphasis added.)

2 Chronicles 13:5 says,

Ought you not to know that the Lord, the God of Israel, gave the kingship over Israel to David forever, even to him and to his sons by a covenant of salt?

Why is the blood of Jesus so important? Because it was foretold in the Holy Scriptures a virgin would give birth to the Son of God (Isaiah 7:14; Luke 1:34-35 and Matthew 1:18) and he would be sent not to condemn the world but rather that the world through Him might be saved (find salvation and be made safe and sound through Him, John 3:16-17). **And because He was the Son of God His blood was *WITHOUT* the Adamic stain of sin.**

The Heavenly Father prepared Him a body that would have blood that was not corrupted by the curse that was released on mankind after the first Adam disobeyed God (Heb. 10:5-10; Genesis 3). So, when this blood was sacrificed through the obedience of Jesus the Heavenly Father received it and reconciled mankind back to Himself (Romans 5:19).

Hebrews 10:5-10 Explains the Reason *God Prepared a Body for Jesus,*

Hence, when He [Christ] entered into the world, He said, Sacrifices and offerings You have not desired, but instead You have *made ready a body for Me [to offer]*;

In burnt offerings and sin offerings You have taken no delight. Then I said, Behold, here I am, coming to do Your will, O God –[to fulfill] what is written of Me in the volume of the Book…Thus He does away with and annuls the first (former) order [as a means of expiating sin] so that He might inaugurate and establish the second (latter) order.

And in accordance with this will [of God], we have been made holy (consecrated and sanctified) through the offering made *once* for all of the body of Jesus Christ (the Anointed One).

In the book, *The Power of the Blood,* the Author further explains how **God the Father Prepared a Body for His Son *with Perfect Blood,*** [1]

His blood was perfect and the Holy Spirit was the Divine Agent who caused Jesus' conception in Mary's womb. This, therefore, was not a normal conception, but a supernatural act of God in planting the life of his already existent Son right in the womb of Mary, *with no* normal conception of a male spermatozoon with the female ovum of Mary. As the blood type of the Son of God was a separate and precious type, it is inconceivable that Mary could have supplied any of her Adamic blood for the spotless Lamb of God. *All the Child's Blood came from His Father in heaven by a supernatural creative act of God.* Jesus' Blood was without the Adamic stain of sin.

The idea by a few that Mary supplied the ovum and that the Holy Spirit supplied the spiritual spermatozoon would mean that Jesus would have been conceived with mixed blood, part of Adam and part of God, which is repugnant to God's plan of salvation for a fallen human race.

The fact of the matter is that God says in the Bible that He prepared a body for His Son. It was that body that was created in Mary's womb.

Jesus' conception was not normal but supernatural. The following is that of a normal conception, [2]

The female ovum itself has no blood, neither has the male spermatozoon; but it is when these come together in the fallopian tube that conception takes place, and a new life begins. *The blood cells in this new creation are from both father and mother* and the blood type is determined at the moment of conception and is thereafter protected by the placenta from any flow of the mother's blood into the fetus.

The reason His blood had to be perfect and not mixed with the first Adam (Paraphrased), [3]

Of course the obvious is that Jesus' blood could not be tainted with the cursed blood if He was to accomplish His mission and He did. Therefore, when God created man, He formed a body from the dust of the ground (Gen. 3:19) – from the substances and chemicals of this planet. Then *He breathed into this body the breath of life.* In other words, He breathed into this chemical composition some of His own spiritual life, and that life was held in the chemical substance we call blood.

So, you see, blood is not life, but it carries life. This becomes quite clear by observing what happens at death. Immediately after expiration, the person is still warm, and will remain so for a brief time. Yet that person is dead because the mysterious *life* has departed from the blood. The life of man is carried in his blood stream. **Life itself is spiritual, but it must have a physical carrier, and this carrier is the blood.** Our blood has the capacity to carry the life of God, the contact between the Divine and the human rests in the blood stream.

Jesus was the only begotten of the Father (John 1:14) and His body was formed and fashioned wonderfully in the womb of Mary His mother; but the Life that was in Jesus Christ came alone from the

Father by the Holy Spirit. No wonder He said I am the LIFE (John 14:6).

When disobedience corrupted the life in our blood it was no longer that pure breath of life from God and it was causing us to die. But because of God's mercy, desire for a family, fellowship, His love for all of us and the assignment to take back the authority in the world from Satan and give it back to mankind to manage, *He sent His only begotten Son.* The result is we can overcome evil by the blood of the Lamb, Revelation 12:11.

To further explain covenants, one must understand there were ceremonies involved to seal them. However, they had to be repeated regularly and for man's sins repeated yearly until the blood covenant put a stop to it forever.

"Covenants were not only concluded with an oath (Gen. 26:28; 31:53; Josh. 9:15), but, after an ancient custom, confirmed by slaughtering and cutting a victim into two halves between which the parties passed, to intimate that if either of them broke the covenant it would fare with him as with the slain and divided beast. Moreover, the covenanting parties often partook of a common meal (Gen. 26:30; 31:54) or at least of some grains of salt." [4]

"According to the Mosaic ritual, the blood of the victim was divided into halves; one-half was sprinkled upon the altar and the other upon the people (Ex. 24:6-8). The meaning of this seems to be that, in the sprinkling of the blood upon the altar, the people were introduced into gracious fellowship with God, and atonement made for their sin. *Through the sprinkling of the blood upon the people Israel was formally consecrated to the position of God's covenant people.*" [5]

Additional Facts Regarding Jesus' Birth

A Sign is Given Regarding the Birth of Jesus in the Old Testament (the Tanakh) in Isaiah 7:14,

> Therefore the Lord Himself shall give you a sign: Behold, the young woman who is unmarried *and* a virgin shall conceive and bear a son, and shall call his name Immanuel [God with us].

This Account of Jesus' Birth is taken from Luke 2:4-7 NKJV,

> Joseph also went up from Galilee, out of the city of Nazareth, into Judea, to the city of David, which is called Bethlehem, because he was of the house of lineage of David, to be registered with Mary, his betrothed wife, who was with child. So it was, that while they were there, the days were completed for her to be delivered. And she brought forth her firstborn Son, wrapped Him in swaddling clothes, and

laid Him in a manger, because there was
no room for them in the inn.

He was born in Bethlehem of Judea as
prophesied in the days of King Herod, Mic. 5:2;
Luke 2:11. Who after finding out from wise men
they were there to worship the King of the Jews and
give Him gifts, King Herod was disturbed about this
and tried to convince the wise men after they located
the Child to share the news with him so he could
worship Jesus too. But he was only plotting to do
harm, Matthew 2:1-10; Ps. 72:10.

When they saw the star (Num. 24:17; Mt. 2:9-
10) that was guiding them they went into the Child's
house who was with His mother, Mary, and they fell
down and worshipped the Child. Then opening their
treasure bags, they presented to Him gifts of gold,
frankincense and myrrh, three different types of gifts
by numerous wise men, Matthew 2:11.

After their visit to Jesus' home the wise men
were divinely instructed and warned in a dream not
to go back to Herod" (Paraphrased Matthew 2:1-12;
Jeremiah 23:5-6; Zech. 9:9; John 19:19.)

What was the purpose of Jesus being born in
Bethlehem? Bethlehem means the House of Bread
(Bethlehem comes from two Hebrew words Beth or
Beit meaning house or household and lechem or le-
chem means bread).

Jesus referred to Himself as the Bread of Life,
John 6:48. Bethlehem is in the region that was part

of the territory given to Judah which represents the kingly line. When Jacob (Israel) was blessing his children, he declared that Judah would be the kingly line. Jesus is from the tribe of Judah which establishes His Kingly line.

Jesus is Revealed in the Old Covenant (Old Testament)

Jesus is revealed from Genesis to Malachi in the Old Covenant (the Tanakh). He is seen in each of the thirty-nine books. Where Salvation is expressed or mentioned it is speaking about Yeshua. Yeshua means Salvation or Savior. He is the Promised One that was sent to save His people. He is the One they expected and that arrived at the appointed time.

In the book of Isaiah, it reveals the sign that was given so the leaders as well as others would know the time of visitation. Isaiah 7:14 says, "Therefore the Lord Himself shall give you a sign: Behold, the young woman who is unmarried *and* a virgin shall conceive and bear a son, and shall call his name Immanuel [God with us]."

Many names are used to describe Him yet His identity is concealed to those that do not know Him. It is concealed from those who cannot see with spiritual eyes or those that do not have divine understanding. This is one reason why Holy Spirit is so important to have in our lives. He is among other things a Revealer. He will bring fresh revelation, truth, an anointing to destroy yokes and cause spiritually blind eyes to see. And with Jesus' teaching of wisdom, understanding will be imparted, Prov. 4:7-9. Yet thousands received Him, however, most of the ancient religious leaders did not.

The Question is Why?

If they were well versed in the scriptures they of all people should have been aware of the Messiah's visitation by the signs, the miracles, and fulfillment of prophecies if nothing else.

Messianic Rabbi Zev Porat of Messiah of Israel Ministries Sheds Some Light and Understanding to their Decision to Ignore and Even Hide Truth about the Visitation of our Lord.

He says, "There are passages in the Tanakh (the Old Testament) that were forbidden to be read by the ancient Rabbis." Their decision and plot have been passed from generation to generation among the Jewish people.

For example, a well-known passage that reveals who the Messiah is has been forbidden by Jews to read. "The forbidden chapter is Isaiah chapter 53. It is speaking about Yeshua being on the cross dying for our sins. How He was led like a lamb to slaughter and He did not open His mouth, then rising up in three days.

This passage was read and proclaimed before Jesus went to the cross and it was eliminated sixty or seventy years after the cross and forbidden by the rabbis. In the synagogue they were not allowed to read Isaiah 52 or 54 because their eyes might wander to Isaiah 53 and this would be dangerous for them. Many were told if they read this passage they could bring a curse on themselves and become sick or die.

The religious leaders believed if the people followed Jesus they would lose their power and authority over the people. Therefore, they set out to try and eliminate the Gospel (the Good News). Not realizing they were entering into spiritual warfare between God and Satan, they had been deceived by the enemy, Satan, and they are operating out of fear of loss. Their actions to try to eliminate truth, by their own testimonies they are saying Yeshua is the Messiah."

Messianic Eitan Bar currently serves as, One for Israel's Director of Media and Evangelism. He is a native of Jewish-Israeli. He too has shed some light on a puzzling question as why Jewish people do not believe Jesus is the Messiah.

He says, "What if Jesus is the best kept secret in Judaism, hidden on purpose from all of us? We all are witnesses of the exclusiveness that the Rabbis created for themselves in their tradition. But this is not something new. It was like that already 2000 years ago."

He continues to say, "Jesus was the only one who dared to stand up against the religious oppression by breaking down the walls that rabbinical tradition had put up. Jesus opened the door to God for everyone: for the simple and for the Gentiles. And so today, thanks to Jesus, millions of Gentiles from all over the world, from different cultures and countries believe in the God of Israel and find a future, hope, comfort, joy and everlasting life in the very same Jew who lived here, in Israel, 2000 years ago."

In the New Covenant (New Testament) it is clearly seen Who the Promised One is! It is clearly revealed that fulfillment of what was spoken in the Old Covenant (Old Testament) has manifested in the pages of the New Covenant.

One Example Spoken about Jesus in the Old Covenant and revealed in the New is Isaiah 9:6-7 where it says,

> For to us a Child is born, to us a Son is given; and the government shall be upon His shoulder, and His name shall be called Wonderful Counselor, Mighty God, Everlasting Father [of Eternity], Prince of Peace. Of the increase of His government and of peace there shall be no end...

He also appeared in the report of Moses and the burning bush, where it states, "the Angel of the Lord is identified as the Lord Himself." (Exodus 3:2 Amplified Bible Footnote). The Angel of the Lord not only appeared and spoke with Abraham but received a meal Abraham and Sarah prepared for Him and two angels that were with him, Genesis 18:1-7.

As a Person in Authority

He is our Savior, our High Priest, the Good Shepherd, our Bridegroom and Eldest Brother. He is the Head of His family as we are His body, His children, His flock of sheep, His bride and we are joint heirs with Him.

While on the earth, He was the Son of God, the Son of man, an Orthodox Jewish Rabbi, a Prophet, our High Priest, a King, a Teacher, Friend, and Oldest Brother, (John 4:42-44; John 18:37; Matt. 13:57; Matt. 21:11; 2 Sam. 7:16; Ps. 89:29).

As King He is our Lord, Master, Commander-in-Chief, Chief Apostle, and Bishop that will rule His Kingdom with justice and might as He leads and instructs His church to govern, legislate and manage His Kingdom on the earth.

Because He is our King and we are a remnant, those true worshippers will live for and in Christ Jesus, in His Kingdom and function as sons of God. They also operate as His partners, mature believers, citizens in His Kingdom, soldiers in His army, as a government (fivefold ministry offices, Eph. 4:11-12) and all those that walk in His authority, John 6:63, Job 28:27-28 and Proverbs 1:1-7.

Jesus Declares His Authority, Matthew 28:18,

Jesus approached and, breaking the silence, said to them, All authority (all power of rule) in heaven and on earth has been given to Me.

Therefore, when you join His Kingdom you walk with the authority that is given in His name, the name that is above every name. Jesus said, "Behold! I have given you authority *and* power to trample upon serpents and scorpions, and [physical and mental strength and ability] over all the power that the enemy [possesses]; and nothing shall in any way harm you, Luke 10:19."

He is the promised "Seed" of the woman that shall bruise the head of Satan, Genesis 3:15; Gal. 4:4. His assignment or mission as a perfect man who never sinned is the "Redeemer" of the lost (those without a covenant shall be saved through Salvation/Yeshua).

Signs and Wonders Follow Jesus and Those with Him

The signs and wonders that followed Jesus then, follow His children now, except greater works will be done in these last days.

We Will Do Greater Works, John 14:12 says,

I assure you, most solemnly tell you, if anyone steadfastly believes in Me, he will himself be able to do the things that I

do; and he will do even greater things
than these, because I go to the Father.

Some of the works Jesus did and Believers
still do today in Jesus' name are: Raise the dead,
heal the sick, open blind eyes and deaf ears, limbs
grow out, the lame walk, broken hearts are healed,
relationships restored and lives are totally
transformed by the power of God.

Believers are experiencing in this time and
age all types of miracles around the world and it will
increase. We will see more miracles (supernatural
moves of God) such as weight supernaturally falling
off people, teeth supernaturally restored, hair
restored and supernatural debt cancellations
occurring. Furthermore, there will be an increase in
the supernatural transfer of real property for homes
and businesses as we progress in this season of
God's glory and harvest.

Marriages are being supernaturally restored
with a renewed love for one another. Families are
restored, prodigals coming home and many barren
women will conceive and have children. People are
being freed from bondage and torment as demons
are cast out of people's lives.

These are just a few of the different types of
recorded miracles that take place around the world
today. Unfortunately, they are seen as threats to
some unbelievers and religious people (all religion
and no personal relationship with God) those who
have chosen the ways of men with their traditions,
customs and embracing religious spirits.

Just as in the days of Jesus, when He walked on water, calmed the wind and sea, or transformed on the Mount of Transfiguration, or restored people who were demon possessed or when he fed five thousand men or four thousand men not counting women or children with a few loaves of bread and a small amount of fish with food left over. Or when He died on a cross on Friday afternoon to become our Passover Lamb and rose from the grave on Sunday morning! People are ready for the miraculous in great measure once again! Mark 6:45-51; Mk 4:39; Mk 9:2-3; Mk 16:17; Mk 1:21-27; Mk 6:32-44; Mk 8:1-13; Mk 15:33-41; Mk 16:1-8.

Some would prefer to receive the glory of men rather than the glory of God. The bottom line is this, Jesus Christ's church will prevail and come forth without spot or wrinkle, as He has said. Therefore, we are to patiently await His return by continuing in Him with His plan and ways going about doing good to advance the Kingdom of God. And in the midst of waiting and continuing in Him we will experience a glorious life like never before. Many will benefit from it as we pray for those who disagree or do not embrace the joy or healing and less suffering in the land but will need a touch from heaven, Mark 1:31, 34; Luke 8:49-55; Rev. 3:10-11; Romans 5:1-5; Matt. 9:1-25.

Jesus is The Last Adam

**I Corinthians 15:45-49 Speaks about the
First Adam and the Last Adam,**

> Thus it is written, The first man Adam became a living being (an individual personality); the last Adam (Christ) became a life-giving Spirit [restoring the dead to life].
>
> But it is not the spiritual life which came first, but the physical and then the spiritual.
>
> The first man [was] from out of earth, made of dust (earthly-minded); the second Man [is] *the Lord* from out of heaven.
>
> Now those who are made of the dust are like him who was first made of the dust (earthly-minded); and as is [the Man] from heaven, so also [are those] who are of heaven (heavenly-minded).
>
> And just as we have borne the image [of the man] of dust, so shall we *and so let us* also bear the image [of the Man] of heaven.

The First Adam's body which was made from dust was formed before God's breath (spirit) entered into him and "created him; male and female, He created them" and thus, "Man became a living being," Genesis 1:27; 2:7.

God "blessed them and named them [both] Adam [Man] at the time they were created," Genesis 5:2. Adam means man or mankind. Later the first Adam changed his wife's name to Eve, Genesis 3:20.

God created the earth for a purpose and suddenly the purpose came alive by His hand. All was created in Him, through Him and for Him, Col 1:16. The purpose for man to be on the earth was to become the bride of Messiah (Christ).

Man (mankind) was someone Christ chose to dwell with on the earth. Someone God could love, fellowship with, have a family (body of Christ, Believers as sons and daughters in the family of God). Someone He could place in position to manage the earth.

In the midst, mankind was deceived and fell, Genesis 3. Since God knows all things, being Omniscient, He already knew the earth and all that was in it would be surrendered to the enemy by the first Adam. He already knew man's disobedience and rebellion would come, and they would fall short of that place of glory they once dwelled in, Romans 3:23.

God already knew when the first Adam fell he would lose his mind (the Hebraic mindset (a mind of God), lose his authority in the earth, and lose the glory that kept him in a position where he could fellowship and walk with God Himself.

Out of God's love and mercy for that which He created from dust, He chose to redeem and restore them into the spiritual place where His glory could rest upon them (male and female) once again.

Romans 5:18-19 NKJV Speaks Clearly of the Results of the First Adam and the Difference in the Outcome of the Last Adam

> Therefore, as through one man's offense *judgment* came to all men, resulting in condemnation, even so through one Man's righteous act *the free gift came* to all men, resulting in justification of life. For as by one man's disobedience many were made sinners, so also by one Man's obedience many will be made righteous.

Once the first Adam fell it made provision for the Last Adam to complete what the first Adam failed to accomplish. The Last Adam, Jesus would be the only One capable of completing the assignment of redemption and reconciliation between Father God and mankind.

In doing so, the earth was introduced to Yeshua HaMashiach, Jesus the Messiah, Himself. The Second Person of the Trinity and the Last Adam Who would redeem mankind forever!

Therefore, all was not lost because God had a plan! He sent the Last Adam, His Son (God incarnate). *By creating Himself in the image of mankind with perfect blood in His veins He redeemed His creation.*

The Last Adam's *spiritual life was in the beginning with God and God made and formed a body for Him*, Hebrews 10:5-10. This was partially done so Jesus' Spirit could legally enter a person on earth. As a human being He gained authority over the enemy and all the earth as His perfect blood, without the Adamic stain of sin was shed at the cross. Authority in His name could also be used by those who received Him, Matthew 28:18.

The Last Adam will reign with all those who are with Him and there will be a new heaven and earth full of the beauty and wonders of God because of the stance, obedience and love of the Last Adam, the Messiah, our Lord and Savior.

Facts About the Genealogy of Jesus the Messiah

"According to the prophecies in the Old Testament, the Messiah must be a descendant of David. In the New Testament Apostle Paul starts his letter to the church in Rome:" [6] Romans 1:3 says,

"[The Gospel] regarding His Son, Who as to the flesh (His human nature) was descended from David."

"In the past, nobody questioned that Jesus was a descendant of David, neither historians nor the Sages. This was because the genealogical scrolls of the people of Israel were accessible in the Temple. If somebody disagreed he would have speedily pointed out the mistake referring to these scrolls.

Everyone knew Jesus was indeed a descendant of David. If Jesus was not from the Davidic line, both the priests and the Rabbis during Jesus' time, not to mention the Talmud, would have pointed this out." [7]

"The Jewish tradition itself states that the Messiah should not have a biological father. We have discussed this matter in detail about the Son of God and the virgin birth of the Messiah." [8]

The New Testament Jesus was in the royal kingly line and the priesthood. Jesus was a descendant of David from both his biological mother, Mary's (Miriam in Hebrew) ancestry, Luke 3:23-38 and Jesus' adoptive father, Joseph, Matthew 1:1-16. "In Judaism an adoptive father was always considered father in every respect." [9]

"Today, we don't have the genealogical scrolls, therefore it is impossible to prove the lineage of any contenders claiming to be the Messiah since the time of the second temple. In Jesus' case, however, the scrolls were still available to be seen, and even the writings of his adversaries prove He fulfilled the criteria. He was indeed from the line of David." [10]

Other facts regarding Jesus the Christ, the Messiah's earthly genealogy tell us more about Who He is. The record of His genealogy is important to fully understand His role in God's redemptive plan.

It is also known Jesus' genealogy was the first mention of a Word from God in four hundred years. Four centuries of silence from the book of Malachi to the book of Matthew until God broke His silence and introduced His plan through His Son's genealogy.

As mentioned earlier, Matthew 1:1-16 speaks of Jesus' Step-father, Joseph's ancestry. The book of Luke 3:21-22 speaks of His True Father and His biological mother's ancestry is recorded in Luke 3:23-38.

In the genealogy of His adoptive father, Joseph, it records forty names and traces Jesus' earthly lineage back some two thousand years over forty-two generations.

The Old Testament spoke of the Coming of Messiah for more than seven hundred years before He was born. In other words, it was seven centuries before the prophecies would be fulfilled. In Isaiah 9:6 it speaks of His kingship and other passages in Isaiah spoke of His being born of a virgin and what His name would be called. Micah 5:2-5 speaks of a Ruler who would be born in Bethlehem.

In Jeremiah 31:22 it speaks about a transformed woman who will embrace the transforming God. Jeremiah also prophesied there would be suffering because of the death of infants around the time of Jesus' birth. King Herod who heard of His coming as an infant tried to destroy Jesus by putting "to death all the male children who were in Bethlehem and in all its districts, from two years old and under, according to the time which he had determined from the wise men. Then was fulfilled what was spoken by Jeremiah the prophet..." Matthew 2:16-18 NKJV.

There were over three hundred prophecies concerning the First Advent (First Coming) of the Lord of which about forty-eight were directly related to the birth of Jesus Christ. The Messiah was the only One who fulfilled all the prophecies said about Himself.

Jesus' genealogy was not the norm. It had all sorts of people ranging from different stations and status in life. There were Jews, kings, foreigners, Gentiles, spies, the poor and the wealthy, prostitutes and military heroes.

His genealogy also included women. In ancient history women were not listed. The five women listed in His genealogy were: Tamar, Rahab, Ruth, Uriah's wife, Bathsheba and Mary. Three of these women were Gentiles.

Therefore, in addition to listing women His genealogy broke the barrier between Jew and

Gentile. The following is a short point about each one of these women.

Tamar was chosen to marry Er, the first-born son of Judah. Now Judah who was married to a Canaanite woman was one of the sons of Jacob. Er acted wickedly by withholding from his wife Tamar and God slew him because of it. Tamar married his brother and he did the same thing and he died also. The father, Judah held his third son from marrying her and later Judah's wife died.

Then sometime after that Tamar disguised herself as a harlot and slept with her father-in-law. In her third month of pregnancy he discovered she was pregnant for him. Her father-in-law said she was more righteous than he because he withheld his third son from her.

Rahab was a Gentile woman, a Canaanite who was also a prostitute who had helped the spies Joshua sent to spy out the land at Jericho. She hid them on the roof and told them when it was safe for them to leave. She also told them she knew their God was the God of heaven.

She informed them the people there were afraid of the Israelites because of the stories they heard of what God had done for them at the Red Sea and their God fighting kings for them. Because of what she did, she and her entire immediate and extended family were spared when the walls of Jericho fell and the city was taken by the Israelites.

She later married a Jewish man named Salmon and their son Boaz married Ruth.

Ruth the Moabitess was loyal to her Jewish mother-in-law, Naomi. Ruth took Naomi's God as her own God when Naomi returned to Bethlehem with Ruth. Later, Ruth as a widow married Boaz and her great grandson became King David.

Bathsheba the daughter of Eliam and the former wife of Uriah the Hittite became the wife of King David after he had her husband murdered in the line of duty while she was pregnant with King David's child. Their first child died but the second one lived and grew and became King Solomon who God made the wealthiest person in the world even to this day and one of the wisest. God also allowed him to build Him a house (temple) to dwell in among the people.

Mary (Miriam in Hebrew) the mother of Jesus (Yeshua) was of course Jewish and known throughout history as a blessed woman. Under her direction Jesus performed His first miracle at a wedding.

Jesus' genealogy also broke the barrier between the saint and the sinner. Those that were in serious sin, in the natural, under the law would have been excluded from worshipping in the temple and being chosen to be in the genealogy of the Messiah.

Those that were considered moral outsiders, or of the wrong culture, those in adultery, those of the female gender, Gentiles, as well as Judah and

David who were moral failures as well, would have been excluded. But now they are being publicly acknowledged as the ancestors of the Lord Jesus Christ.

People that were excluded because of their culture, their race, the law of Moses or society in general can be brought into the family of God. It really does not matter who or where you are from or what you have done. If you repent (change your mind and go in His direction doing things His way) and believe in Him the grace of Jesus Christ can remove your sin, if that is the case for your exclusion and reunite you with Him.

Furthermore, if it is because of culture and man-made rules as to why you have been excluded, Jesus will welcome you into His Kingdom where love, forgiveness, favor, blessings and opportunities are in the abundance.

One last point regarding His genealogy, it begins and ends with a supernatural birth. Abraham whose son was a miracle baby and at the end of the line was Jesus, also a miracle baby who was born of a virgin. This ended the long wait for the Messiah who came at the appointed time and Who is *Coming Again!*

The Genealogy of Jesus the Messiah in Matthew 1:1-17,

Vs. 1-2

> The book of the ancestry (genealogy) of Jesus Christ (the Messiah, the Anointed), the son (descendant) of David, the son (descendant) of Abraham. Abraham was the father of Isaac, Isaac the father of Jacob, Jacob the father of Judah and his brothers...

Vs. 16-17

> Jacob the father of Joseph, the husband of Mary, of whom was born Jesus, Who is called the Christ. (the Messiah, the Anointed) So all the generations from Abraham to David are fourteen, from David to the Babylonian exile (deportation) fourteen generations, from the Babylonian exile to the Christ fourteen generations.

I Am the Door

So, as you seek to find your way, find it in Jesus. He said, "I assure you, most solemnly I tell you, that I Myself am the Door for the sheep," John 10:7. He is the way through whatever your dilemma. He has the answer and the way to overcome and conquer whatever the situation you are presented with.

He is the Door. He is the Connection between heaven and earth. Wherever Jesus is, heaven is open. Jesus is an open portal to heaven. He said, "I am the Door."

When He came to earth as the Son of God He still had the mind of heaven. Even though He dwelled on earth in human form as a mere man He still had a voice because He belonged to heaven. He knew who He was and only did what He saw the Father doing and He did nothing of Himself, John 5:19.

We were made in God's image. Possessing His Spirit, His character, His incarnate human features. Because He is the Door, if we are Born-again, we are seated in heavenly places with Him as He is seated at the righthand of the Father, Eph. 2:6 and Mark 16:19.

We have favor and receive intercession from Jesus Himself. We have angelic assistance and divine wisdom is imparted for strategies we may need for daily living. We can walk by faith and receive the abundant life God gave us as He helps us defeat our enemies.

He is the Door to whatever we need. He opened the way for us to do what He does and say what He says. In doing so we will be Christ-like and receive the higher life He left for us. Why? Because we are a door as well. We have the same authority He has as we declare His Name.

Opportunities will present themselves, favor will go out before us and Holy Spirit will guide us into all truth.

We can exercise our agreement with heaven and stay aligned by following the Word of God, the Bible, our instruction manual. We will learn as we feed on the Word and confess what it says (speak it out loud). We have Holy Spirit to ensure we go through the right doors and not miss God's timing. He will also make sure the wrong doors are closed in our lives.

If we remain with Him, knowing who we are in Messiah, speaking the word in faith (taking action and believing before we see manifestations) our words will not return to us void.

As we exercise our authority on the earth with the mind of Christ, heaven and earth are connected and the heavens will move things on the earth on our behalf.

As we are seated with Christ we will learn to deal with opposition from a place of rest. We are seated, seated represents a place of rest. Rest is trusting God will do what we cannot do and overturn wrong things until they turn for our good. The test is, do you believe it? If so, get ready for breakthroughs as you rest in Messiah and continue going forward.

Jesus is Our Joy

When Jesus is our Joy, He will be our strength. Joy brings strength into our lives. Jesus has pleased and glorified the Father. Jesus is our covering and Redeemer. Therefore, when Father God sees us He does not see the flaws, shortcomings, mistakes or sin when we ask for forgiveness and repent.

What Father God sees is Jesus and what He did to bring us in a position where we could come boldly to the throne of God with our love, fellowship and requests. He sees Jesus' integrity, purity, sacrifice, love, His hope for us – He sees the family and friendship He desires to have with us. He sees warriors that will take back what was stolen from His Kingdom.

As God sees Jesus, as He is righteous, He sees me as righteous. As God the Father sees Jesus as holy, He sees me as holy, special and set apart for His enjoyment and purpose in His Kingdom.

He sees me and loves me the more because of the Joy Messiah brought to earth and back to heaven. Therefore, "Rejoice in the Lord always.

Again, I will say rejoice!" Phil. 4:4; Ro. 5:3 NKJV. Refuse to let the enemy, Satan steal your joy and peace with circumstances, financial issues or relationship problems.

Know by faith you have already won. Know by faith you are seated with Him in a place where full authority is at your fingertips. Know by faith you won't have to fight in this battle because the battle is not yours but the Lords, 2 Chron. 20:15-25. So, rejoice in the Lord, focus on Him and not your problems and stay Happy!

Everything is going to be alright because, He is "the Holy One, the True One, He Who has the key of David, Who opens and no one shall shut, Who shuts and no one shall open," Rev. 3:7; Isaiah 22:22. In You, Lord my God, I put my trust, Psalm 25:1.

Chapter 3

The Commission Sent from Heaven

Jesus was sent from Heaven to earth to reconcile people back to Father God after the fall of mankind, Genesis 3. They would be reconciled through salvation. Salvation was obtained by the shedding of His perfect blood to make a Covenant that would redeem mankind forever from the curse that was set in the earth after the fall.

He Claimed Identity with the Father in their Unique Trinitarian Relationship as the One Who Sent Him, Matthew 12:44-50 says,

> But Jesus loudly declared, The one who believes in Me does not [only] believe in and trust in and rely on Me, but **[in believing in Me he believes] in Him Who sent Me. And whoever sees Me sees Him Who sent Me. I have come as a Light into the world,** so that whoever believes in Me [whoever cleaves to and trusts in and relies on Me] may not continue to live in darkness. If anyone hears My teachings and fails to observe them [does not keep them, but disregards them], it is not I who judges him. *For I have not come to judge and to condemn*

and to pass sentence and to inflict penalty on the world, but to save the world. Anyone who rejects Me and persistently sets Me at naught, refusing to accept My teachings, has his judge [however]; for the [very] message that I have spoken will itself judge and convict him at the last day. This is because *I have never spoken on My own authority or of My own accord or as self-appointed, but the Father Who sent Me has Himself given Me orders [concerning] what to say and what to tell.* And I know that His commandment is (means) eternal life. So whatever I speak, I am saying [exactly] what My Father has told Me to say and in accordance with His instructions. (Emphasis added.)

The Forerunner of Jesus was the Spirit of Elijah

Jesus was announced by the spirit of Elijah through John the Baptist. John the Baptist was a prophet in the wilderness. He was filled with the Spirit of God while in his mother Elizabeth's womb. She was a descendant of Aaron and His father belonged to the priestly division of Abia, and both of his parents were considered righteous in the sight of God, Luke 1:5-6.

His mother was barren, and both of his parents were advanced in age. One day while his father was on duty serving as priest, an angel of the Lord appeared to him and told him his wife Elizabeth would have a son and he was to call this child John, Luke 1:11-13. He also told him his son would be filled with Holy Spirit before he was born and he was given other instructions as well. Luke's purpose for recording this was he wanted the full truth understood by the people who had been orally taught, Luke 1:4.

John's purpose is written, that "he will [himself] go before Him in the spirit and power of Elijah, to turn back the hearts of the fathers to the children, and the disobedient *and* incredulous *and* unpersuadable to the wisdom of the upright [which is the knowledge and holy love of the will of God] – in order to make ready for the Lord a people [perfectly] prepared [in spirit, adjusted and disposed and placed in the right moral state]" Luke 1:17; Mal. 4:5, 6.

When Mary the mother of Jesus also with Child went to visit Elizabeth in the hill country to a town of Judah, (Luke 1:39) when she came into her presence and greeted her the baby within Elizabeth leaped inside of her and Elizabeth was filled with the Holy Spirit, Luke 1:41.

The Prophet Isaiah was a Voice for the Lord as said in Isaiah 40:3,

A voice of one who cries: Prepare in the wilderness the way of the Lord [clear away the obstacles]; make straight *and* smooth in the desert a highway for our God!

"...The Word of God came to John the son of Zacharias in the wilderness. And he went into all the region around the Jordan, preaching a baptism of repentance for the remission of sins, as it is written in the book of the words of Isaiah the prophet, saying: The voice of one crying in the wilderness: Prepare the way of the Lord..." Luke 3:2-4 NKJV.

The People were in Expectation and John Answered them Concerning the One Coming, Luke 3:15-16,

As the people were in suspense *and* waiting expectantly, and everybody reasoned *and* questioned in their hearts concerning John, whether he perhaps might be the Christ (the Messiah, the Anointed One).

John answered them all by saying, I baptize you with water; but He Who is mightier than I is coming, the strap of Whose sandals I am not fit to unfasten. He will baptize you with the Holy Spirit and with fire.

Jesus On Earth as the Son of God

When Jesus walked the earth as the Son of God He was fully God and fully man. Yet He had to be anointed for His assignment because He literally had emptied Himself and made Himself of no reputation (poured Himself out) and took upon Himself the form of a servant. Furthermore, because He was made in the likeness of men He had to do things by the power of Holy Spirit.

Philippians 2:7 tells us He Humbled and Positioned Himself,

But stripped Himself [of all privileges and rightful dignity], so as to assume the guise of a servant (slave), in that He became like men *and* was born a human being.

Because of what was made possible through Jesus, once again Father God could communicate with His creation. Mankind can once again fellowship in a personal relationship with God because we were fully reconciled to Him.

Jesus showed us how to communicate with Father God through Him and how to walk by faith.

He was a living example. He was the Way as an example and as a breaker through barriers no one else could achieve.

"God sent Moses as the mediator of His covenant, but as great as Moses was, he was merely a servant in God's house. Jesus is the Son (Heb. 3:5-6), the Mediator of the new and final covenant (Heb. 8:6). He comes with a message of judgment for those who will not repent, but he has grace and mercy for all who come to the Father through Him. He intercedes for us before the Father's throne, and he invites people from all nations –men and women, young and old – to receive the blessings of the new covenant. In Him, and through Him, we are able to enter God's presence and dwell with Him forever, (NLT Parallel Study Bible)."

It is Further Recorded in Hebrews 8:7-8, 10 NKJV,

> For if that first *covenant* had been faultless, then no place would have been sought for a second. Because finding fault with them, He says: "Behold, the days are coming, says the LORD, when I will make a new covenant with the house of Israel and with the house of Judah... I will put My laws in their mind and write them on their hearts; and I will be their God, and they shall be My people.

In addition, mankind will also be able to be restored and to take back from Satan what was captured on the earth by his lies. The fallen angel, Lucifer whose name became Satan after he lost his way and fell from heaven because of pride and rebellion (Isaiah 14:12-15) is now doomed to the Lake of Fire, his final place of abode.

He and all evil spirits including the anti-Christ that followed him and unfortunately the human beings who have been deceived by his lies and did not believe in the One who was sent to save them from outer darkness will all be together in the Lake of Fire for eternity with Satan Rev. 20:14-15.

However, the Good News is Christ entered legally through a human by birth and successfully accomplished His mission. Christ Jesus gained access with full authority to operate in the earth and His followers, Believers, have the same authority to do so, Matthew 28:18.

He made it clear Who He was and identified Himself in the scrolls, the Bible in the Old Testament (The Tanakh) for all to hear, *then He sat down.*

Jesus Read Isaiah 61:1-3 and Spoke about *His* Mission on Earth,

THE SPIRIT of the Lord God is upon me, because the Lord has anointed *and* qualified me to preach the Gospel *of* good tidings to the meek, the poor, *and* afflicted; He has sent me to bind up *and* heal the brokenhearted, to proclaim liberty to the [physical and spiritual] captives and the opening of the prison *and* of the eyes to those who are bound,

To proclaim the acceptable year of the Lord [the year of His favor] and the day of vengeance of our God, to comfort all who mourn, (Also see Luke 4:18-19.)

To grant [consolation and joy] to those who mourn in Zion – to give them an ornament (a garland or diadem) of beauty instead of ashes, the oil of joy instead of mourning, the garment [expressive] of praise instead of a heavy, burdened, *and* failing spirit –that they may be called oaks of righteousness [lofty, strong, and magnificent, distinguished for uprightness, justice, and right standing with God], the planting of the Lord, that He may be glorified.

After Identifying Himself in the Word of God Jesus Sat Down, Luke 4:20 says,

> Then He rolled up the book and gave it back to the attendant and sat down; and the eyes of all in the synagogue were gazing [attentively] at Him.

Sitting down indicated He acknowledged the assignment and was at rest. He knew Who He was and Who to trust in to accomplish all He needed to do while on the earth as the Son of God.

In Isaiah 61:1 it explains *the Messiah was sent* (apostles are the sent ones). Jesus was sent as an Apostle. He also operated as a Preacher and High Priest, Isa. 61:1 and Heb. 3:1-3. Inspired preachers are also known as Prophets. Jesus also functioned as a Prophet, Mt. 21:11; Mt. 13:57; Eph. 4:11. Furthermore, He taught in the synagogues as a Master Teacher (Rabbi), Luke 4:14-16. He went about healing and doing good. He also became the Pioneer of our Salvation which is key in Evangelism, Heb. 2:10. So, in essence Jesus operated in all of the fivefold ministry gifts which is the structure He began for His church.

He Came to Lay His Life Down, Jesus Predicts His Death

There are people on the earth, Christian and non-Christian, who have persecuted the Jewish people out of ignorance of not knowing or receiving the whole truth about Christ's death. They say the Jews murdered Jesus when in fact, Jesus came to lay His life down and conquer death.

The part the Jewish leaders had in the plan of God (unknown to them) led to Jesus' death which in turn gave eternal life for all who believe. Without His death we all would have been sentenced to hell because we would not have had a Savior to die and conquer by taking the keys to death, hell and the grave, Revelation 1:18.

The truth is, His body was prepared with perfect blood, blood that did not carry the Adamic curse which was the result of the fall, Genesis 3.

He was sent on a mission by Father God to redeem and reconcile mankind back to the Father. This would entail conquering the curse of death. To remove the curse of death it required the death of a sinless person. Therefore, in His death, He took every curse that was placed on mankind from the beginning in the Garden to the end of time.

Jesus (Yeshua) shed His blood that would redeem all of mankind forever. It formed a blood covenant that could never be broken. In doing so He gave the victory to all those who believe and receive.

He Speaks of His Death in Mark 8:31 and 32,

And He began to teach them that the Son of Man must of necessity suffer many things and be tested *and* disapproved *and* rejected by the elders and the chief priests and the scribes, and be put to death, and after three days rise again [from death].

And He said this freely (frankly, plainly, and explicitly, making it unmistakable).

Again, He Speaks of His Death in Luke 21-23 NIV,

Jesus strictly warned them not to tell this to anyone. And he said, "The Son of Man must suffer many things and be rejected by the elders, the chief priests and the teachers of the law, and he must be killed and on the third day be raised to life." Then he said to them all: "Whoever wants to be my disciple must deny themselves and take up their cross daily and follow me.

The Book of Isaiah 53:1-12 (Yesha 'Yahu 53 in Hebrew) Not Only Confirms the Messiah was Sent to the Earth But Through Prophecy Confirms that His Death Would Take Place as Seen Below,

1. WHO HAS believed (trusted in, relied upon, and clung to) our message [of that which ways revealed to us]? And to whom has the arm of the Lord been disclosed?

2. For [the Servant of God] grew up before Him like a tender plant, and like a root out of dry ground; He has no form or comeliness [royal, kingly pomp], that we should look at Him, and no beauty that we should desire Him.

3. He was despised and rejected *and* forsaken by men, a Man of sorrows *and* pains, and acquainted with grief *and* sickness; and like One from Whom men hide their faces He was despised, and we did not appreciate His worth *or* have any esteem for Him.

4. Surely He has borne our griefs (sicknesses, weaknesses, and distresses) and carried our sorrows *and* pains [of punishment], yet we [ignorantly] considered Him stricken, smitten, and afflicted by God [as if with leprosy].

5. But He was wounded for our transgressions, He was bruised for our guilt *and* iniquities; the chastisement [needful to obtain] peace *and* well-being for us was upon Him, and with the strips [that wounded] Him we are healed *and* made whole.

6. All we like sheep have gone astray, we have burned every one to his own way; and the Lord has made to light upon Him the guild *and* iniquity of us all.

7. He was oppressed, [yet when] He was afflicted, He was submissive *and* opened not His mouth; like a lamb that is led to the slaughter, and as a sheep before her shearers is dumb, so He opened not His mouth.

8. By oppression and judgment He was taken away; and as for His generation, who among them considered that He was cut off out of the land of the living [stricken to His death] for the transgression of my [Isaiah's] people, to whom the stroke was due?

9. And they assigned Him a grave with the wicked, and with a rich man in His death, although He had done no violence, neither was any deceit in His mouth.

10. Yet it was the will of the Lord to bruise Him; He has put Him to grief *and* made Him sick. When You *and* He make His life an offering for sin [and He has risen from the dead, in time to come], He shall see His [spiritual] offspring, He shall prolong His days, and the will *and* pleasure of the Lord shall prosper in His hand.

11. He shall see [the fruit] of the travail of His soul and be satisfied; by His knowledge of Himself [which He possesses and imparts to others] shall My uncompromisingly] righteous One, My Servant, justify many *and* make many righteous (upright and in right standing with God), for He shall bear their iniquities *and* their guilt [with the consequences, says the Lord].

12. Therefore will I divide Him a portion with the great [kings and rulers], and He shall divide the spoil with the mighty, because He poured out His life unto death, and [He Himself] be regarded as a criminal *and* be numbered with the transgressors; yet He bore [and took away] the sin of many and made intercession for the transgressors (the rebellious).

What He came and did for all humanity goes beyond words. Not only do we receive eternal life because of His humble act, but while on the earth we receive forgiveness for all past, present and future sins. Our sins are forgiven throughout eternity as we align with Him. All He offers can become a reality in our lives.

For example, in verse four where it says our griefs, is translated to: He took our sicknesses, weaknesses, and distresses. Sorrow is related to taking our pain. He suffered what we should have suffered before we die. And if we were in sin without a Savior at the time of death the sentence was to the pit and then the Lake of Fire forever, Revelation 20:10. But in His mercy and grace He took it all, including eternal death and gave us life.

In verse five where it says He was bruised, it is speaking about the thirty-nine stripes He took on His back from the Roman soldiers. These thirty-nine stripes represent every major disease in the earth. Therefore, we can receive healing for our sickness and relief when we are afflicted.

In the New Testament it also clarifies His death. In the book of Matthew while Jesus was still on the cross in the ninth hour (three o'clock) He cried out twice and the second time with a loud voice and gave up His spirit, Matt. 27:46-50.

Matthew 27:51-54 Gives Us Details about what Occurred After Jesus Gave Up His Spirit,

> And at once the curtain of the sanctuary of the temple was torn in two from top to bottom; the earth shook and the rocks were split. The tombs were opened and many bodies of the saints who had fallen asleep in death were raised [to life]; And coming out of the tombs after His resurrection, they went into the holy city and appeared to many people. When the centurion and those who were with him keeping watch over Jesus observed the earthquake and all that was happening, they were terribly frightened *and* filled with awe, and said, Truly this was God's Son!

He is our Deliverer from all curses. There is a threefold curse in effect (spiritual death; sickness; poverty and debt), Deut. 28:15. We as children of God are to be spared from curses because God gives blessings not curses, Deut. 28:2. He is the Anointed One and the anointing can *destroy* the yoke of bondage, Isaiah 10:27 NKJV.

We are to resist evil as it tries to come upon us and weigh us down, James 4:7. Redemption is threefold (new birth; healing; and divine Holy Spirit prosperity). (See *God's Way and Finances* to review the prosperity God has for those who have chosen Him.)

His Resurrection

Resurrection is the day the Messiah, Jesus the Christ rose from the dead by the power of Holy Spirit. He was crucified as our Passover Lamb, I Cor. 5:7, "In Whom we have our redemption *through the blood,* [which means] the forgiveness of our sins," Col. 1:14. Furthermore, we received eternal life at the time we received salvation when we were Born-again (saved). Eternal life continues after we pass from this life into glory.

Jesus Declared He is the Resurrection, John 11:25-26,

Jesus said to her, I am [Myself] the Resurrection and the Life. Whoever believes in (adheres to, trusts in, and relies on) Me, although he may die, yet he shall live; And whoever continues to live and believes in (has faith in, cleaves to, and relies on) Me shall never [actually] die at all. Do you believe this?

At the time of passing our spirit man returns to heaven, each of us will receive a glorified body and at the appointed time we will return to earth with the Lord. We will live forever in the presence of the Lord, I Cor. 15:42-44; Phil. 3:20-21.

In addition, "He also is the Head of [His] body, the church, Eph. 1:22; seeing He is the Beginning, the Firstborn from among the dead, so that He alone in everything *and* in every respect might occupy the chief place [stand first and be preeminent]," Col. 1:18.

He was sent to earth by Father God and the Word of God says, "Do not think that I have come to do away with *or* undo the Law or the Prophets; *I have come not to do away with or undo but to complete and fulfill them,"* Matthew 5:17. After fulfilling His mission and assignment from Father God, Yeshua (Jesus) became our Redeemer, Lord, Savior, High Priest and Friend.

Ancient Jews also believed in the Third Day Resurrection. The Apostle Paul was able to demonstrate the Messiah would rise from the dead on the third day. In Acts 17:2-3 it tells us, "And Paul entered, as he usually did, and for three Sabbaths he reasoned *and* argued with them from Scriptures. Explaining [them] *and* [quoting passages] setting forth *and* proving that it was necessary for the Christ to suffer and rise from the dead, and saying, This Jesus, Whom I proclaim to you, is the Christ (the

Messiah)." [1]   In the book of 1 Corinthians 15:4 it states very clearly "that He was buried, that He arose on the third day as the Scriptures foretold."

Further Details Regarding the Resurrection in I Cor. 15:20-23,

> But the fact is that Christ (the Messiah) has been raised from the dead, and He became the firstfruits of those who have fallen asleep [in death]. For since [it was] through a man that death [came into the world, it is] also through a Man that the resurrection of the dead [has come]. For just as [because of their union or nature] in Adam all people die, so also [by virtue of their union of nature] shall all in Christ be made alive. But each in his own rank *and* turn: Christ (the Messiah) [is] the firstfruits, then those who are Christ's [own will be resurrected] at His coming.

It was also shown in Psalm 22 and Isaiah 53 the Messiah would be killed but would rise afterwards.

In John 19:34 the Bible Records Proof of Death,

> But one of the soldiers pierced His side
> with a spear, and immediately blood and
> water came (flowed) out.

Today we have the technology to know when a human being dies the blood in their body separates into serum: a transparent liquid like water and red blood cells. John probably included this passage not knowing it would be a major scientific factor in proving the Messiah had indeed died.

And since He was seen by hundreds of witnesses over the next forty days it is safe to say He rose from the dead in three days like He said He would. "God is not a man, that He should tell *or* act a lie..." Number 23:19.

Hosea 6:1-2 Also Gives an Example of Ancient Israel being Aware of a Third Day Resurrection,

> COME AND let us return to the Lord, for
> He has torn so that He may heal us; He
> has stricken so that He may bind us up.
> After two days He will revive us
> (quicken us, give us life); on the third
> day He will raise us up that we may live
> before Him.

The book of Esther has a three day fast in the face of annihilation which also gives the theme of death and resurrection. Her life was spared by the king when the truth of what the adversary planned was told by Queen Esther 4:14-16; Esther 7.

Again, in the book of Jonah it too has the theme of three days and three nights. As he was in the belly of a large fish prepared by the Lord to swallow him and three days later vomit him out onto dry land. He was then ready to complete the mission the Lord had sent Him to do, Book of Jonah.

This story was confirmed in the New Testament as well, "For even as Jonah was three days and three nights in the belly of the sea monster, so will the Son of Man be three days and three nights in the heart of the earth," Matt. 12:40.

After Jesus rose from the grave having taken back the keys to death, hell and the grave and before His ascension into heaven He walked the earth for forty (40) days. He was seen by as many as five hundred (500) people at once, I Cor. 15:6. He appeared to His disciples many times in that 40-day period. He spent time in the forty days teaching the apostles and disciples about the Kingdom of God, Acts 1:3.

On the first day after He rose from the grave the first person He appeared to was a woman, Mary Magdalene, John 20:11-19; Matt. 28:9-10. Later that same day He appeared to His disciples who were behind closed doors because they were afraid of the

Jewish leaders. He said unto them "Peace to you," John 20:19. "He showed them His hands and His side. And when the disciples saw the Lord, they were filled with joy (delight, exultation, ecstasy, rapture)," John 20:20.

He proceeded to send them forth just as Father God sent Him forth. So, "He breathed on them and said to them, Receive the Holy Spirit," John 20:21-22. He also appeared to two disciples going to a village called Emmaus about seven miles from Jerusalem and spoke with them. They did not know who He was until evening when they broke bread together and their eyes were opened and then Jesus vanished before them, Luke 24:13-31.

In Luke 24:33-44, it gives another account of one of His visits. He appeared to all eleven apostles which included Peter, others who were with them and the two male disciples on the road Jesus spoke to earlier and said to them "Peace." They were afraid and terrified at first and thought they had seen a spirit, but He spoke with them and showed them His hands and feet and told them to handle or feel Him to see it was really Him. He told them "see, for a spirit does not have flesh and bones, as you see that I have." He also showed them His hands and feet.

"And while [since] they still could not believe it for sheer joy and marveled, He said to them, Have you anything here to eat? They gave Him a piece of broiled fish, And He took [it] and ate [it] before them," Luke 24:41-43.

Eight days later Thomas was in the house with the apostles and others. He refused to believe them when they shared with him that Jesus was alive. He could not believe them and would need to see Jesus himself in order to believe. Jesus appeared to them while Thomas was present and said, "Peace to you!" Jesus told Thomas, "Reach out your finger here, and see My hands; and put out your hand and place [it] in My side... *[stop your unbelief and] believe! Thomas answered Him, My Lord and my God*," John 20:26-28.

Blessed are Those Who Believe *Before* They See, John 20:29,

Jesus said to him, Because you have seen Me, *Thomas,* do you now believe (trust, have faith)? Blessed *and* happy *and* to be envied are those who have never seen Me and yet have believed *and* adhered to *and* trusted *and* relied on Me.

He also appeared to James then all the apostles, I Cor. 15:7. "Now the eleven disciples went to Galilee, to the mountain to which Jesus had directed *and* made appointment with them," Matt. 28:16.

In John 21:1-12 Jesus appeared to Peter and the others as they had been out fishing and caught nothing. He was on the shore and told them to let their net down on the right side, they did and they caught a huge catch. John said to Peter, "It is the Lord!" And Peter jumped into the sea to go ashore. Jesus had even prepared breakfast for them as they came in. He gave them bread and fish. This was the third time He had revealed Himself to them after He had risen from the dead.

His Ascension

The ascension completed His time on earth as the Son of Man. His ascension was forty (40) days after the Resurrection and ten (10) days before Pentecost a total of fifty (50) days. Jesus gave instructions when He was about to ascend. He told them "And behold, *I will send forth upon you what My Father has promised;* but remain in the city [Jerusalem] until you are clothed with power from on high," Luke 24:49. That power would come from the Holy Spirit in the upper room on the day of Pentecost (Shavuot), Acts 2:1-4.

He further explained about the power they would receive saying, ***"But you shall receive power when the Holy Spirit has come upon you;*** and you shall be witnesses to Me in Jerusalem, and in all Judea and Samaria, and to the end of the earth," Acts 1:8 NKJV.

In the meantime, "When He had spoken these things, ***while they watched, He was taken up, and a cloud received Him out of their sight.*** And while they looked steadfastly toward heaven as He went up, behold, two men stood by them in white apparel, who also said, "Men of Galilee, why do you stand gazing up into heaven? This *same* Jesus, who was taken up from you into heaven, will so come in like manner as you saw Him go into Heaven," Acts 1:9-11 NKJV; Luke 24:50-51.

When the Lord "was taken up into heaven, He sat down at the right hand of God," Mark 16:19 NKJV. "And they worshipped Him, and returned to Jerusalem with great joy, and were continually in the temple praising and blessing God," Luke 24:52-53 NKJV.

The Word of God further says, "they went out and preached everywhere, the Lord working with *them* and confirming the word through the accompanying signs," Mark 16:20 NKJV.

The Lord Assured Them He Would be Returning for Them, John 14:2-3,

> In My Father's house there are many dwelling places (homes). If it were not so, I would have told you; for I am going away to prepare a place for you. And when (if) I go and make ready a place for you, I will come back again and will take

you to Myself, that where I am you may be also.

The King is Coming for a Glorious Church!

What God is doing in this hour is going to require **His Glory to unlock**, to release or transfer and bring forth to the rightful owner things that have been held back from their generational bloodline for centuries. During the End-Times, God said we would do greater works than He, John 14:12. He also said, apart from Me you can do nothing, John 15:5.

Furthermore, it all will begin with the Releasing of His Glory that is appointed for this hour and scheduled according to His timing to come upon the earth in greater strength like never before. We will witness things we have never seen or heard of before.

Jesus Prayed to be Glorified, John 17:1-5 NIV,

"Father, the hour has come. Glorify your Son, that your Son may glorify you. For you granted him authority over all people that he might give eternal life to all those you have given him. Now this is eternal life: that they know you, the only true God, and Jesus Christ, whom you have sent. *I have brought you glory on earth by finishing the work you gave me to do. And now, Father, glorify me in your presence with the glory I had with you before the world began.* (Emphasis added.)

The King of kings is prepared to glorify His church. He said, "I have given to them the glory *and* honor which You have given Me, that they may be one [even] as We are one: I in them and You in Me, in order that they may become one *and* perfectly united, that the world may know *and* [definitely] recognize that You sent Me and that You have loved them [even] as You have loved Me.

Father, I desire that they also whom You have entrusted to Me [as Your gift to Me] may be with Me where I am, so that they may see My glory, which You have given Me [Your love gift to Me]; for You loved Me before the foundation of the world," John 17:22-24.

When God's will is perfectly accomplished, manifestation on the earth is supposed to look like heaven. It will be His glory on the earth.

After His Ascension, Jesus was Reinstated and Totally Restored to Majesty and Honor. It says in Hebrews 1:2-3,

> "[But] in the last of these days He has spoken to us in [the person of a] Son, Whom He appointed Heir *and* lawful Owner of all things, also by *and* through Whom He created the worlds *and* the reaches of space *and* the ages of time [He made, produced, built, operated, and arranged them in order]."

> Verse 3 NIV, *"**The Son is the radiance of God's glory and the exact representation of his being, sustaining all things by his powerful word.** After he had provided purification for sins, **he sat down at the right hand of the Majesty in heaven.**"* (Emphasis added.)

The fact Jesus was glorified indicates He was prepared and empowered to release glory to His church. This paved the way for His return as King over a glorious church.

The King is Coming, Zech. 9:9-10,

> Rejoice greatly, O Daughter of Zion! Shout aloud, O Daughter of Jerusalem!

Behold, your King comes to you; He is [uncompromisingly] just and having salvation [triumphant and victorious], patient, meek, lowly, and riding on a donkey, upon a colt, the foal of a donkey.

And I will cut off *and* exterminate the war chariot from Ephraim and the [war] horse from Jerusalem, and the battle bow shall be cut off; and He shall speak the word and peace shall come to the nations, and His dominion shall be from the [Mediterranean] Sea to [any other] sea, and from the River [Euphrates] to the ends of the earth!

King Jesus' power will be manifested in the Kingdom of God as the church operates once again in their true identity and authority. As the church functions as it did in the Early Church, God's power will manifest His Glory.

The glory, His tangible *Presence* will be ushered in by His glorious church. With compassion and love for the people, wisdom and strength will come from His Spirit and creative miracles, signs and wonders and key breakthroughs for your life will be the result of His glorious Presence.

We must understand *we the church carry the Glory of God!* Each Believer as a part of the Body of

Christ is the true church, Eph.1:22-23. As we know, when a person is Born-again (Romans 10:9-10; John 3:1-3) they are adopted and grafted into God's family, Eph. 1:5; Romans 11:17-19; Gal. 3:24. And the church is characterized by the fivefold ministry gifts for the perfecting of the Saints for the work of ministry, Eph. 4:11-16.

So, as we carry the Glory of God it is vital for a Christian Believer to know their "true identity," knowing who they are in Christ! What is equally important to release, are godly positive words that will release life, faith and angels. Remember, death and life are in the power of the tongue, Prov. 18:21.

Words are containers of power and are spirit. The right words spoken, godly words which align with God release power and the glory of God is manifested.

Exactly how is the glory of God manifested in and through us? The glory, the blood and our spirit (heart) are all aligned and wrapped together in us. The Spirit of God flows through our blood (the life from our Spirit is in the blood) and the glory flows through the Spirit.

The glory God has for this season will have extreme favor connected to it, power will be connected to it, clarity and hearing Holy Spirit will be even greater as you spend time in His presence. As the glory comes from heaven it will be connected to the glory that is already in you.

The glory of God is His manifested tangible Presence. Therefore, God will manifest Himself in a **tangible Presence** in such a way you can perceive Him with your physical senses. *In other words, you can see, hear, smell, taste and touch His Presence.*

In God's Presence His visitations or manifestations can cause crying, seeing visions, hearing God's voice in your spirit man, falling under the power of God, shaking, sensing warmth somewhere on your body, smelling perfume in a room or place where there was none prior, hearing a pop somewhere on your body, or feeling something that reminds you of electricity. You can experience an instant healing and any form of something supernatural occurring when He manifests His glory.

This is wonderful but how does one taste His Presence? Psalm 34:8 says, "O taste and see that the Lord [our God] is good!" When you take refuge in Him you taste it by seeing the harvest, the blessing, the fruitfulness, and participating in His wonderful covenant!

To grow and mature as sons and daughters and deepen your relationship and experience His glory there are a few things you need to press forward into. Such as, Believers should be baptized in and built up by Holy Spirit; trained and equipped with the Word of God; walk in the fruit of the Spirit; the gifts of the Spirit activated in their life; God's spiritual weapons of warfare exercised; walking with a spirit of boldness; and exercising faith! (In the next paragraph I have added scriptures for reference and personal study.)

Believers should be baptized in and built up by Holy Spirit *(Mark 1:8; Acts 2:1-4; Mt. 4:4; Jude 1:20; John 6:63);* trained and equipped *(Eph. 4:11-12)* with the Word of God *(John 1:1; Ps. 1:1-3; Isa. 55:11; I Sam. 30:6);* walk in the fruit of the Spirit *(Gal. 5:22-23);* the gifts of the Spirit activated in their life *(I Cor. 12:7-11);* God's spiritual weapons of warfare exercised *(Mt. 11:12; Eph. 6:12; I Peter 5:8-10);* walking with a spirit of boldness *(Acts 4:29);* and exercising faith *(Heb. 11:6, 8; Col. 1:4)!*

In this time, the Lord is restoring what was lost from His church. The church lost its power during the Dark Ages. The church has been robbed of the Kingdom of God which has with it the power to rule. The church has been watered down, lied to and heavily persecuted since the Dark Ages. It lacks confidence and faith and many live in fear, sickness, poverty, guilt and condemnation which affects their faith. This is still happening today!

But now the season has changed! There has been a shift. *Restoration is here and God is restoring the glory to a greater level than the church had before it was robbed of the glory.* A greater level because we will do greater works. The fivefold ministry gifts are coming into place and operating through Apostolic, Prophetic Centers. This will also *go beyond the church walls because it is for people in the marketplace as well.*

With full confidence and assurance knowing who we are in Christ, we shall walk in full authority as we confront the enemy and remind him he is already a defeated foe. *Great works will be accomplished in these End-Times to set the captives free by the glorious church for its King of Glory.*

Wherever Jesus encountered Satan's work or devices in operation He destroyed it. Where He saw people sick, He healed them, if possessed with unclean spirits, He set them free. If they were broken hearted and depressed He brought hope and joy into their lives and if they were hungry He fed them by the thousands, Matt. 14:13-21; Mt. 15:29-39.

All the things He did plus more, Jesus has assigned to His glorious church. Believers are called to manifest God's Kingdom on earth in the midst of Satan's territory. God is giving territory to its rightful owners. Territory is not only restricted to land. It is whatever God has given you dominion (authority) over. This would include your person (your body), your home, work place, your city, wherever He causes your feet to thread you have been given His authority. His glorious church is to walk in His authority, power and faith and do greater works than He did in His humanity, Mt. 28:18, John 14:12.

Therefore, the fivefold ministry gifts will be used by God to tear down old structures that work in conjunction with the enemy's kingdom, Isa.

61:1; Isa. 10:27. As God works through the Saints/Believers, they will be equipped to bring the presence of God on the scene to do the work only God Himself can do. As God works through us we will bring salvation to lost sinners, heal the sick in every area of their lives including sick finances, sick relationships and so much more for the people's sake.

We will impart prosperity in areas where they were robbed. By giving them or confirming what the Lord is doing in their lives. Divine wisdom will be imparted with strategies that will out think the enemy so wholeness will come and they can experience supernatural peace, Phil. 4:7.

As Believers, we are to renew and transform our minds, so we no longer think religion but think Kingdom. God is enlarging our territory as we take back what belongs to His Kingdom (government) away from the world's system (government).

The church began on Pentecost in an upper room when Holy Spirit came in and baptized one hundred and twenty men and women as they were filled with Holy Spirit and began to speak in other languages (tongues), Acts 2:1-4. The foundation the Early Church had was rooted in the Torah. Through the Torah God shaped their lives daily.

Through God's teachings He taught the Jewish people His ways from holiness and His character, righteousness, repentance, foods that were clean and unclean to the difference between sin and what it means to be set apart, special and used by God. They were taught giving tithes and offerings as well as participating in appointed times of meeting with Him for His appointed feasts.

They were also taught by the fivefold over time to operate in the gifts of the spirit where they would prophesy and see miracles of healings and all sorts of manifestations from the Spirit of God. However, the biggest thing they were introduced to was the New Covenant that was written on their hearts by Almighty God, Jeremiah 31:31-33; Matthew 26:26-29.

Messiah came for the Jews first to form a priestly people who would then go to the nations and teach them God's ways Romans 1:16. The fivefold ministry gifts were introduced to the new Believers as followers of Messiah. They experienced profound results as the Early church saw great miracles with signs and wonders. They were filled with the Spirit of God and operated in the gifts of the Spirit.

It is time for the church to become Kingdom minded and walk in wisdom, leadership roles, health, abundance and over-all well-being that was given to us at the cross.

We gained everything as Christ gave up everything when He laid His life down for us. (See *Chapter Seven* for the things He gave so we could be whole.) We can at last receive what He did for all of us, Jew and Gentile in Messiah (Eph. 2:14-20).

This is a time of restoration and God is not only restoring government in the land, your homes, families, businesses but He is restoring *His church.*

He is bringing the church back to where it is supposed to be – a powerful Kingdom that ushers in God's plan and will take good care of its citizens.

Believers must broaden their mentality past traditional church thinking to having a Kingdom mindset. An apostolic mindset is in those who are sent to be the breakers that will break you into the new. They are sent to change and shape the culture. Our Apostolic model is Jesus/Yeshua. The apostles are not afraid to live and walk in the spirit, deal with spiritual enemies and are accustomed to seeing the supernatural/miracles and victorious results.

So, allow His Holy Spirit to work through the fivefold ministry gifts, angelic forces as well as use spiritual gifts to empower you to do a work in this season that will prepare a people to be ready for when the King returns for His glorious church.

Be the light God called and intended each and every one of us to be in order to bring comfort and hope to those trapped in the kingdom of darkness. As we do, we will manifest God's goodness and love on the earth, and experience the promises He has given us, Ps 103:1-22.

Nevertheless, some backbone with a spirit of boldness to confront the enemy's devices (poverty, lack, sickness, divorce, brokenness, scattered families, strife, rebellion, unforgiveness, bitterness, depression and on and on) in your life in the name of Jesus. He who is with you along with the power of Holy Spirit and the angels that are assigned to help you will take it all back for His glory, in Jesus' name.

Jesus is also the Lord of Hosts, YHVH Tsabaoth. He is the Commander of the armies of heaven. The Lord of Angels, the very help God has sent to bring you into what He has for you in this season. Angels are a part of the Hosts and make up the armies of Heaven. They are the supernatural army standing against the powers of darkness in the first and second heavens.

Angels were very common in the Early Church when God's church exercised great power seeing signs and wonders, miracles, healings and the dead raised. Angels provide for the people of God amid suffering persecution, I Kings 19:5-8.

Just as they did then they are beginning to do now in this new season. Holy Spirit will dispatch angels in these Last Days to work with and for the Believers to bring them into victory. As we continue to move forward in faith, praying and speaking God's Word at the appointed time(s) God will command His angel armies out to ensure our victory.

He is returning for a glorious church! However, He sent a warning for His people before

His return. He also told His church to watch and pray so they would be prepared for His coming.

He said to Watch for His Coming Luke 21:34-36 NKJV says,

> But take heed to yourselves, lest your hearts be weighed down with carousing, drunkenness, and cares of this life, and that Day come on you unexpectedly. For it will come as a snare on all those who dwell on the face of the whole earth. *Watch therefore, and pray always that you may be counted worthy to escape all these things that will come to pass,* and to stand before the Son of Man. (Emphasis added.)

The Messiah's Return

He came into this world a Jew through a miraculous birth. He laid His life down and died a Jew and on the third day rose from the grave a Jew Who was and is the Son of God. He will return as "the Lion of the tribe of Judah, the Root (source) of David..." Rev. 5:5.

Titles by which He will be called at His return will be "The Word of God" Rev. 19:13 and on His thigh He has a name (title) inscribed, King of kings and Lord of lords, Rev. 19:16.

He is now our High Priest (Hebrew 4:15) and at His Second Coming, Christ will set up the Davidic mediatorial kingdom and reign as King-Priest (Zech. 6:11-13; Rev. 19:16; Matt. 2:2; I Tim. 1:17).

The Messiah Will Build the True Temple, Zech. 6:12-13,

> And say to him, Thus says the Lord of hosts: [You, Joshua] behold (look at, keep in sight, watch) the Man [the Messiah] whose name is the Branch, for He shall grow up in His place and He shall build the [true] temple of the Lord. Yes, [you are building a temple of the Lord, but] it is He Who shall build the [true] temple of the Lord, and He shall bear the honor *and* glory [as of the only begotten of the Father] and shall sit and rule upon His throne. And He shall be a Priest upon His throne, and the counsel of peace shall be between the two [offices-- Priest and King].

The Messiah Jesus as prophesied, will walk or visit certain regions upon His return. It is written in Ezekiel where the prophet speaks of the glory of the

Lord passing through the Eastern or the Golden Gate in Jerusalem.

Ezekiel 43: 2 says,

> And behold, the glory of the God of Israel came from the east and His voice was like the sound of many waters, and the earth shone with His glory.

Also, in the book of Zechariah it speaks of the Messiah's feet standing on the Mount of Olives facing Jerusalem on the east side when Jesus (Yeshua) returns as He is going forth to fight nations that will come against Jerusalem.

Once done Yeshua will pass through the ancient Kidron Valley and re-enter through the Eastern or Golden Gate of Jerusalem as the *King of kings!*

The Lord's Feet Shall Stand Upon Mount of Olives, Zec. 14:4 says,

> And His feet shall stand in that day upon the Mount of Olives, which lies before Jerusalem on the east, and the Mount of Olives shall be split in two from the east to the west by a very great valley; and half of the mountain shall remove toward the north and half of it toward the south.

The Lord Shall be King Over All the Earth, Zec. 14:9,

And the Lord shall be King over all the earth; in that day the Lord shall be one [in the recognition and worship of men] and His name one.

Jerusalem Shall be Secure, Zec. 14:11,

And it shall be inhabited, for there shall be no more curse *or* ban of utter destruction, but Jerusalem shall dwell securely.

Those Left that Came Against Jerusalem Shall Worship at God's Feast, Zec. 14:16

And everyone who is left of all the nations which came against Jerusalem shall even go up from year to year to worship the King, the Lord of hosts, and to keep the Feast of Tabernacles.

Worship Will Involve God's Feasts

Being in His will, will align you with God and you will be able to make the right connections to move forward into your purpose which will advance the Kingdom of God. However, it will require that we are willing and obedient, Isa. 1:19 NIV says, "If you are willing and obedient you will eat the good things of the land."

To help us stay in the timing of God we must follow the biblical calendar God placed in the earth. His Feasts are His appointed times to meet with us for worship. In turn we receive blessings, divine wisdom, strategies, protection, and so forth for our willingness to do things His way.

Most Jews presently observe seven feasts. *Three of them are appointed times God has set to meet with mankind forever.* The three main feasts are Passover, Pentecost and Tabernacles. The seven feasts consist of "The Passover, Unleavened Bread, Firstfruits, Pentecost, Trumpets, Atonement and Tabernacles. *The first four have been fulfilled literally by Jesus.* He was the Passover Lamb (I Cor. 5:7), the Bread of Life (John 6:35) and the firstfruits of those who have fallen asleep (I Cor. 15:20). And when Pentecost had fully come after His ascension, He sent us the Holy Spirit (Acts 2:1-4)." [2]

"So the next feast we are waiting for Jesus to fulfill literally is the Feast of Trumpets…" When the trumpet sounds, 'in the twinkling of an eye,' we who are alive will be changed. We will put on new bodies that will be like Jesus' body! Those who are dead in Christ will rise and also receive new bodies. They will go up first followed by us who are alive, and we will all meet the Lord in the air" (I Cor. 15:51-55)." [3] The catching away of the church is also referred to as the rapture of the church (the Body of Christ and/or the One New Man, Eph. 2:14-16).

These are God's feasts designed for appointed times known as Moed. These appointed times are for the people to meet with God in worship and to bring offerings for His house, Deut. 16:16-17, Mal.3:6-8. The purpose of the feasts commemorates God's faithfulness and reminds us of the many miracles of deliverance He did for His people in ancient times as He set apart Israel as His own people. *Glory to God in the Highest, and on earth, peace, good will toward men! Luke 2:13-14.*

The feasts serve to remind God's people of His holiness, their own impurity and the fact God still wants and desires for His people to meet with Him at His appointed times in spite of any impurities.

Furthermore, the beauty of this is, as Believers in Yeshua/Jesus celebrate the feasts it completes the purpose God intended from the beginning of giving us *The One New Man*, Jew and Gentile, both in Christ/Yeshua as one body of people in God worshipping He alone as the Most High God.

Each of God's feasts reminds us of a specific historical event in ancient days but it also reveals His plan of redemption and points directly to the Messiah Jesus. Therefore, these feasts are relevant to every Believer on the earth.

We thank the Lord and decree the structure of the fivefold ministry that was stolen from Jesus' church will be restored now during this new church age through the One New Man (Believers – Jew and Gentile in Christ).

The Kingdom of God in turn will continue to advance and it will be to the *Glory of the King of kings*. It is His hour and time to reveal His glory, restore, recover and make new. It is harvest time for those who can believe!

Psalm 145: 10-13 NKJV Speaks of God's Kingdom,

> All Your works shall praise You, O LORD, And Your saints shall bless You. They shall speak of the glory of Your Kingdom, And talk of Your power, To make known to the sons of men His mighty acts, And the glorious majesty of His Kingdom. Your kingdom *is* an everlasting kingdom, And Your

dominion   endures   throughout   all
generations.

Chapter 4
The Gift, His Anointing Abides in You

The Anointing Power of God, the Gift of Holy Spirit

The Word of God says, "But you shall have power (ability, efficiency, and might) when the Holy Spirit has come upon you..." Acts 1:8. One definition of the *anointing* is, it is the power of God on your life to enable you to do things you could not ordinarily do or to even receive some things that would be impossible without the anointing to handle it.

An anointed or spiritual family functions according to the Word of God as they choose to live a Christian (Christ-like) lifestyle. The word Christian also means the anointed ones. To further understand what it means to be in the Family of God, operating as such we must first understand the meaning of these terms. The Bible says, "In all your getting, get understanding" (Proverbs 4:7 NKJV) and it tells us for a lack of understanding or knowledge, people will be destroyed Hosea 4:6.

Therefore, it is extremely important to have a clear understanding of who you are so when you confess to be something, you should at least know what it means so you can take a strong stance for what you believe or do not believe to be true in your heart.

I John 2:27 Speaks About the Anointing that Dwells in Us,

> But as for you, the anointing (the sacred appointment, the unction) which you received from Him abides [permanently] in you; [so] then you have no need that anyone should instruct you. But just as His anointing teaches you concerning everything and is true and is no falsehood, so you must abide in (live in, never depart from) Him [being rooted in Him, knit to Him], just as [His anointing] has taught you [to do].

The Definition for the Anointing as given in Vine's Complete Expository Dictionary (Paraphrased) says,

> Believers (Christians, people who are Christ-like) have "an anointing from the Holy One" indicates that this anointing renders them holy, separating them to God. The Holy Spirit is the all efficient means of enabling believers to possess knowledge of the truth.
>
> Thou shalt take of the oil of the anointing, in Ex. 30:25, etc.; it is spoken of as **"a holy anointing oil."**

Masah "to anoint, smear, consecrate." A common word in both ancient and modern Hebrew, masah is also found in ancient Ugaritic. The basic meaning of the word, however, is simply to "smear" something on an object. Usually oil is involved, but it could be other substances.

The Old Testament most commonly uses masah to indicate "anointing" in the sense of **a special setting apart for an office or function. Christ as the Anointed of God signifies "The Anointed One"** (Luke 4:18 and Isaiah 61:1). Also the anointing of Prophets, Priests and Kings; Elisha was anointed to be a prophet (I Kings 19:16); David refused to harm Saul because Saul was "the Lord's Anointed" (I Sam.24:6). Jesus "...formed us into a Kingdom, kings (a royal race) and priests to His God and Father..." Rev. 1:6.

Vessels used in the worship as the sacred shrine (both tabernacle and temple) were consecrated for use by "anointing" them (Ex. 29:36; 30:26; 40:9-10). (Emphasis added.)

Therefore, Christ "The Anointed One and His Anointing" came to live inside of us when we became Christians because we are the "anointed-ones."

Jesus Acquired the Anointing through God, Acts 10:38,

...God anointed and consecrated Jesus of Nazareth with the [Holy] Spirit and with strength and ability and power; how He went about doing good and, in particular, curing all who were harassed and oppressed by [the power of] the devil, for God was with Him.

The Anointing is within you. He is the Holy Spirit helping you with His power that will enable you to do things in God's love and with His strength you could not do on your own. *The Anointing is from God and it is only for covenant people.*

Dr. Joyce Meyer Adds Revelation Regarding the Anointing (paraphrased),

"I do not have anything to offer people except the anointing (presence and power) ...I must have God's anointing in order to do what He has called me to do ...*I have learned that I will not carry God's anointing if I do not walk in love, because God does not anoint the flesh* (our own desires and selfish attitudes or behaviors). God does not anoint carnal behavior. We really must walk in love because that aids and increases the anointing on our lives, and the anointing is what empowers us to do what God has called us to do. God's anointing is His presence and power and it enables us to do with ease what we could never accomplish with any amount of struggle on our own. We all need God's anointing... We need it to be good parents, to have successful marriages, to be good friends, and literally in everything we do." [1]

Through His anointing we are given authority and might. Our anointed family is brought to victory because of the anointing acquired through Salvation and acknowledging God, Prov. 3:6. **There are different kinds, different levels and measures of the anointing,** therefore, even though we have authority (John 1:12) we will not walk in certain levels of power until we become a mature Christian (male or female) who are called sons of God.

They trust in the Lord with all their heart and lean not on their own understanding... In all their ways they know, recognize and acknowledge Him, and allow Him to direct and make straight and plain their paths, Proverbs 3:5-6. True sons of God also honor the Lord with their capital and sufficiency from righteous labors and with the firstfruits of all their income, Proverbs 3:9.

In addition, mature anointed children of God will welcome and receive the Lord's discipline and correction, "…for whom the Lord loves He corrects, even as a father corrects the son in whom he delights," Prov. 3:11-12. Therefore, mature Christian Believers will speak with "skillful *and* godly Wisdom which is more precious than rubies… Length of days (long life) is in her right hand and in her left hand are riches and honor, Prov. 3:13-16. (Emphasis added.)

"And because you [really] are [His] sons, God has sent the [Holy] Spirit of His Son into our hearts, crying, Abba (Father)! Father!" Galatians 4:6. **As sons of God begin to live your life as an heir of God through Christ** and inherit all the blessings of God Jesus inherited as a result of the finished work He accomplished at the cross. This includes your salvation, healing, wholeness, favor, prosperity, prayers answered at the appointed time as well as a personal relationship with God.

Remember an heir of God through Christ also means you are joint-heirs with Jesus, Romans 8:17. The Word of God says, "But it is God Who confirms *and* makes us steadfast *and* establishes us [in joint fellowship] with you in Christ, and has consecrated *and* anointed us [enduing us with the gifts of the Holy Spirit];" 2 Cor. 1:21. These gifts will place us in a position to handle the power that comes with the anointing on higher levels or dimensions placed on our lives as we grow in Him.

One of the Symbols of the Anointing is the Anointing Oil

The Bible says in Psalms 23:5, "…You anoint my head with oil; my [brimming] cup runs over." "He also made the holy anointing oil [symbol of the Holy Spirit] and the pure, fragrant incense, after the perfumer's art" Ex. 37:29. Throughout the Bible the anointing oil was used for powerful times of ministry Mark 6:13.

The anointing is God's burden-removing, yoke-destroying power. The yoke is the "device" that keeps you clamped to your burden. Isaiah 10:27 KJV says, *"And it shall come to pass in that day, that his burden shall be taken away from off thy shoulder, and his yoke from off thy neck, and the yoke shall be destroyed because of the anointing."* This passage declares what happens when the anointing (oil) is used.

The oil in and of itself has no power but when used in accordance with the Word of God it releases your faith. As you pray in **Jesus' name that gives your prayer authority** and it will release the anointing (power) of God into your situation that is **within the will of God.**

The anointing oil is also used when laying hands on the sick. It says once anointed and the prayer of faith goes forth they will be "saved him who is sick, and the Lord will restore him (raise him up); and if he has committed sins, he will be forgiven" (James 5:14-15). Note: if you do not have oil with you and you wish to pray for someone you are "anointed" so go forth and pray and the anointing will still be released. Using anointing oil and laying hands is one way of praying for the sick, for there are other ways. Seek Holy Spirit to show you what you should do at any given moment. It will be more effective than following a routine.

The holy anointing oil was also used to consecrate people for higher office as they were appointed by God Psalm 89:20-21. In the Old Testament the holy oil was poured over heads of prophets, priest and kings as well as vessels and objects inside the tabernacle and temple, I Kings 19:16.

In the book of Isaiah 61:1 Jesus located Himself in the scriptures as He announced in the synagogue "The Spirit of the Lord God is upon Me, because the Lord has *anointed* and qualified Me to preach the Gospel..." It is written in the New Testament as well, "The Spirit of the Lord [is] upon Me, because He has anointed Me [the Anointed One, the Messiah] to preach the good news (the Gospel) ..." Luke 4:18. As He was confirmed to be anointed we are anointed as well because His Holy Spirit dwells in us.

In the New Testament we see the disciples and apostles using the oil to anoint and pray for the sick. Therefore, the practice of using the anointing oil was extended beyond the use of only anointing prophets, priest and kings; it is for whoever desires to benefit from this type of consecration. In both the Old Testament and the New Testament one way the anointing could be transferred was by the laying on of hands Deut. 34:9 and Mark 16:18.

Furthermore, anyone is Born-again has the right to use blessed holy oil. You do not have to wait for leadership from the church to bless your oil (extra virgin olive oil) or for you to anoint and bless your home, business, bank accounts, work place or pray for a sick family member or any other person. In Mark 16:16 it says, "He who believes..." and in vs. 18 it says "...they will lay their hands on the sick, and they will get well." David anointed himself (2 Samuel 12:20).

Anyone and anything anointed is set apart for God's purpose and use. The Holy Spirit Who is The Teacher of all things (John 14:26) is represented in I John 2:27 as it speaks about the "Anointing" Who is God the Holy Spirit. It says, "...you must abide in (live in, never depart from) Him [being rooted in Him, knit to Him], just as [His anointing] has taught you [to do].

Some Believers Do Not Receive the "The Infilling of Holy Spirit" nor do they Desire to be Sons of God

Many Believers settle to be "saved and no more." Reading the Word of God, especially when filled to the brim with His Spirit you will receive deeper revelation of the mysteries found in God's Word. When you are not renewing your mind (Romans 12:2) and you have stopped seeking, asking, expecting, and have stopped your fellowship with God you will start to decrease or lose spiritual ground (we grow in the spirit to different levels as we continue with God) you have received from Holy Spirit and the Kingdom of Heaven.

As ways of the world begin to increase in you and manifest in your life, this may leave you with a form of religion having no real authority or power.

2 Timothy 3:5 says,

> For [although] they hold a form of piety (true religion), they deny and reject and are strangers to the power of it [their conduct belies the genuineness of their profession]. Avoid [all] such people [turn away from them].

"The Holy Spirit distinctly and expressly declares that in latter times some will turn away from the faith, **giving attention to deluding and seducing spirits and doctrines that demons teach,** through the hypocrisy and pretensions of liars whose consciences are seared..." I Timothy 4:1-2. This will hinder and choke off the anointing you received with salvation from flowing in your life and being of benefit to you.

Seduction requires two parties a seducer and someone to seduce. *When you are participating with unholy alliances you have opened a door for the seducer to lead you astray and away from the anointing of God.*

Protect the Anointing on Your Life

God gives us liberty, 2 Cor. 3:17 NIV says, "Now the Lord is the Spirit, and where the Spirit of the Lord is, there is freedom." Freedom always gives us a choice in how we will move forward. We have been set free by God, so we can fulfill our destiny and purpose by following His will and plan for our lives.

We are free to move forward and take our place in the world God destined for us and advance the Kingdom of God wherever we are planted. He says the Truth will set us free, John 8:32. "So if the Son liberates you [makes you free men], then you are really *and* unquestionably free, John 8:36."

Never Allow Your Freedom to be an Excuse to Do Evil, I Peter 2:16,

[Live] as free people, [yet] without employing your freedom as a pretext for wickedness; but [live at all times] as servants of God.

Many of us have been set free from old destructive habits, lifestyles, bondages, addictions, unforgiveness, bitterness, generational curses, tormenting spirits, lack, poverty, and all sorts of things related to condemnation or shame.

The Gift of God's anointing is what destroys yokes, Isa. 10:27. Believers are anointed with His power to successfully move forward in areas of their lives where they have been prepared and equipped to do so. But in doing so we must have the wisdom and knowledge to protect the anointing God has placed on our lives.

One Way to Protect the Anointing of God is Seen in, I Peter 2:13-15,

> Be submissive to every human institution *and* authority for the sake of the Lord, whether it be to the emperor as supreme, or to governors as sent by him to bring vengeance (punishment, justice) to those who do wrong and to encourage those who do good service. For it is God's will *and* intention that by doing right [your good and honest lives] should silence (muzzle, gag) the ignorant charges *and* ill-informed criticisms of foolish persons.

"A godly response to those in authority over you provides you with spiritual safety. *If you submit to authority for the sake of honoring God and His Word, you will enjoy a free flow of His anointing in your life.* If you rebel and refuse to submit, you will block the anointing. Submission protects you from demonic attack, while rebellion opens the door for the enemy. You protect the anointing on your life realizing God has given it to you to help you in all that you do. Remember that things are accomplished by the Spirit of God and not by might nor by power (Zech. 4:6), therefore, to guard your anointing (be obedient); stay peaceful and calm; be quick to forgive, slow to anger, patient and kind. (There are other things) that also protect your anointing but by doing these few things your anointing will be stronger" (Emphasis added). Excerpt from Ending Your Day Right by Dr. Joyce Meyer.

We know submission is basically giving honor and respect to those delegated authorities God has placed in our lives. However, when an authoritative figure (an individual, a party, a government, a state, a city, etc.) is not submitting themselves to the *Will of God*, then and only then are you at liberty to rebel against their authority and go with the Word of God mainly because *God is the final Authority* and the One that is given the highest respect and honor and the only One who can back up and follow through with His Word.

Guard Against Unholy Alliances and Protect the Anointing on Your Life

As listed in Ephesians 4 beginning with verse 25: *Lying* - which has become a lifestyle for many Believers. *Anger* - anger is an emotion not a sin, it can become a sin if we sin while angry. If you go to bed angry you give the devil opportunity to come in. *Stealing* - for example: taking supplies from work, not really working as you should but still expecting full pay, or you receive an overpayment from a cashier and you say nothing and leave. Also, there are Believers who refuse to give tithes and offerings and therefore are robbing God Himself and His house, Malachi 3:8-9. ***Corrupt Communication*** - which proceeds out of your mouth is not only foul language but doubt in God's Word or ability. It is also negative, murmuring and complaining words or speech that is counter to the Word of God.

Satan fears the anointing on the lives of Believers. He knows he is no match for Christ. When he comes with his devices of unholy alliances (example of those spirits listed above and the following: strife, bitterness, slander, gossip, being offended, self-pity, jealousy, depression, lust and suicidal spirits) realize they are sent to quench or stop the anointing on your life from flowing and to hinder your spiritual growth.

All a Believer has to do is release "God's Word in faith" which is an "Anointed Spirit" in the name of Jesus and it will destroy the yoke or device at the root. Remember godly words are containers of spiritual power for a Born-again Christian.

In the Book of Psalms 20:6 it says, "Now I know that the Lord saves His anointed; He will answer him from His holy heaven with the saving strength of His right hand." In Psalm 105:15 it says, "Touch not My anointed, and do My prophets no harm." I have quoted these two scriptures to show ***God knows how to protect His own and He will.***

One way of protection is for Him to first instruct His children, His sons and daughters, on how to live before Him in such a way they stay out of harm's way and are fruitful and prosperous, John

15:16. When others are deliberately trying to harm you, He will protect you for He will avenge His own, Romans 12:19. He also gives a strong word or a warning to those outside of His family when they choose to harm His chosen, Genesis 12:3.

A note to Believers: Are you aware people can operate in the anointing and still sin? *But if they do not repent they cannot continue to operate in the glory of God.* Born-again Christians need the glory of God to stand and remain righteous for this latter season or age God has transitioned people into, Haggai 2:7-9; Psalm 24:6-7. We know the anointing is for every Believer and it will keep your mind (I Cor. 2:16) and give you understanding and the revelation of the mysteries of God that are in His Word. But *the glory of God is designed to protect you.* The anointing will still work in a corrupt person as it works in a person of honor because you can be anointed without the glory of God being on your life.

He was trusted with all levels of authority and power. *When we walk in His righteousness as sons of God* (male or female, because this is a spiritual term and there is no gender in the spirit) *it will bring the glory on our lives* as well. We can be trusted with higher levels of authority and His power because of the glory. Walking in His righteousness simply means, we have been made right by an act of God's grace and mercy. His Holy Spirit dwells in us.

Therefore, God the Father sees Jesus' righteousness and by that we are counted righteous because we are in Him and He is in us. His righteousness gives us a new way of living through our faith in Christ Jesus.

Second Corinthians 5:21 NKJV Speaks of His Righteousness,

> For He made Him who knew no sin *to be* sin for us, that we might become the righteousness of God in Him.

His righteousness supersedes having only an anointing to do a work. Therefore, some people have authority but no power.

Furthermore, *there is a greater power coming to the earth* no one has stepped into yet that will have such awesome miracles, many have never seen before and the time is very, very close. Why do I mention this? Because we are in an hour (a time) where these words are about to come to pass. Jesus says *if anyone believes in Him, "he will himself be able to do the things that I do; and he will do even greater things than these..."* John 14:12.

Someone demonstrated what it would be like to have the glory and an anointing using this illustration: "When the first Adam lived in the garden before the fall of man he had the glory of God on him and he operated by divine revelation and did not really need the anointing to understand God's Word." As mentioned earlier, the anointing may differ, have different levels and measures to the anointing.

Therefore, we want to always strive to draw near to God knowing Him by having a personal relationship with Him. Staying close to God and walking in His righteousness (His way of doing and being right) will enable His glory to come upon our lives in greater measures and work with the anointing in us to do even greater works for the Kingdom of God, Matthew 6:33.

Why are Anointed People Persecuted?

From the beginning of Christianity, Christians have been persecuted not only for following the Anointed One but because they themselves are anointed at the time they receive their salvation. Christ(ian) means Christ (like), we are persecuted because His Spirit dwells in us. The unbeliever's spirit, those not Born-again and some with a spirit of religion, only practicing rituals, traditions and customs and/or a spirit of anti-Christ recognizes the Spirit of God in the Christian who is a Believer in Christ Jesus (Yeshua HaMashiach).

The unbeliever's spirit is no comparison for the anointing, which is Christ, Who displays the true power of Almighty God. "Because He Who lives in you is greater (mightier) than he who is in the world," I John 4:4. The world (unbelievers) hated Him and they will hate you. In addition to this, instead of embracing the miracles and good works that followed Jesus, they hated Him for it. Even today when miracles and good works are done in the name of Jesus by His sons and daughters in faith who operate in the fruit and gifts of God, they are hated and persecuted for it as well.

Jesus said in John 15:18-20; 24-25,

> **If the world hates you, know that it hated Me before it hated you.** If you belonged to the world, the world would treat you with affection and would love you as its own. But because you are not of the world [no longer one with it], but I have chosen (selected) you out of the world, the world hates (detests) you. Remember that I told you, A servant is not greater than his master [is not superior to him]. **If they persecuted Me, they will also persecute you;** if they kept My Word and obeyed My teachings, they will also keep and obey yours. If I had not done (accomplished) among them the works which no one else ever did, they would not be guilty of sin. But [*the fact is*] *now they have both seen [these works] and have hated both Me and My Father.* But [this is so] that the word written in their Law might be fulfilled, **They hated Me without a cause.** (Emphasis added.)

Furthermore, this leads to *the suffering Christians endure because of their stance for Christ. The suffering for Christ does not entail sickness, poverty and tragedies, those things are sent from the enemy and Christians are to resist those forms of evil,* James 4:7. The kind of suffering Believers encounter from others in the world is called persecution and it may first entail hatred towards their Messiah, Jesus Christ. It would also include hatred towards them because they receive and are committed to Him.

True Christians are hated because they are not of this world but of another Kingdom and a part of God's Family. They are hated because they take a stand for Israel and they are hated because people of the world are jealous of what they have in Christ. Many of them detest Christian Believers and pursue them aggressively with the intent to destroy them, and so forth, (I Peter 4:12-19; Luke 6:22; I John 3:13).

Because Believers are hated by those who do not know Father God their names are slandered, they are lied upon, betrayed, left out of events, isolated and separated from others. Some try to make them feel ashamed of the Gospel and what they believe because they have chosen to embrace Truth. But know this, *they are protected by God.* ***He knows how to take care of His own, Psalms 91:1-16.*** They are loved and blessed.

God Protects His Own, Psalm 91:9-11, 15,

Because you have made the Lord your refuge, and the Most High your dwelling place, There shall no evil befall you, nor any plague *or* calamity come near your tent. For He will give His angels [especial] charge over you to accompany *and* defend *and* preserve you in all your ways [of obedience and service].

He shall call upon Me, and I will answer him; I will be with him in trouble, I will deliver him and honor him.

Furthermore, the persecution may vary as stated and vary from country to country. Some being more severe than others. ***People of God have the power and authority to resist harsh treatment.*** God has given us authority to deal with it. If we cannot handle it quietly, forgiving others and moving on then we have no choice but to resist evil and cast it down (James 4:7 and Luke 10:19). (See *God's Way and Spiritual Warfare* to enhance your knowledge of your rights and authority over evil spirits (forces) and gain victory for your family and yourself.)

When Christians maintain their love for others, choosing to forgive in spite of the persecution, they grow closer to God. They also receive an inner joy and God's favor on their lives, Luke 6:21. They become more anointed to walk in His glory and do mightier works, John 17:22-23.

However, they can and should confront when led by Holy Spirit. It is not necessary to fight in every battle. That is a tactic by the enemy to wear the saints out. We can choose our battles and we can choose to forgive all.

This is what is meant by a Believer taking up his cross and following Jesus. As you continue to love the Lord and choose to forgive those who persecute you, you are strengthened with faith and a force of patience working on the inside of you that will enable you to stand until your answer or instructions come, Mark 11:25; 2 Thess. 1:4. This act can also be referred to as dying to your flesh (yourself) and taking on Christ and the anointing.

When you take the position to stand bold, stay strong in Him and focused you are counted as a blessed person, "When a man's ways please the Lord, He makes even his enemies to be at peace with him" and he is rewarded in heaven, Prov. 16:7.

We are Blessed even when Persecution, Luke 6:22-23,

> Blessed (happy – with life-joy and satisfaction in God's favor and salvation, apart from your outward condition – and to be envied) are you when people despise (hate) you, and when they exclude *and* excommunicate you [as disreputable] and revile *and* denounce you and defame *and* cast out *and* spurn

your name as evil (wicked) on account of the Son of Man.

Rejoice *and* be glad at such a time and exult *and* leap for joy, for behold, your reward is rich *and* great *and* strong *intense* and abundant in heaven; for even so their forefathers treated the prophets. (Also see Mt. 5:11-12.)

He will also honor you as you make a conscious decision to take a stand, and not be moved from your position of righteousness but remain rooted and grounded in His love, His Word, truth, faith and patience. As you continue to, spread the Good News (Gospel) that salvation is available; to bless others; to pray for others; and not allow persecution to distract you and cause you to be taken off course from your mandate from God, He will give you the strength and wisdom you will need in order to continue in Him to cross your finish line reaching your destiny and receive the prize (to be supremely blessed, I Peter 4:14).

Chapter 5

His Love, a More Excellent Way

The Bible tells us we are to "earnestly desire *and* zealously cultivate the greatest *and* best gifts *and* graces (the higher gifts and the choicest graces). And yet I will show you a still more excellent way [one that is better by far and the **highest of them all – love**]," I Corinthians 12:31.

Allow Your Life to Lovingly Express Truth, Ephesians 4:15

Rather, let our lives lovingly express truth [in all things, speaking truly, dealing truly, living truly]. Enfolded in love, let us grow up in every way *and* in all things into Him Who is the Head, [even] Christ (the Messiah, the Anointed One).

It is love that seeks the best interest of an individual while seeking nothing for itself in return. The Word says God showed us that example through His act of sending His only beloved Son Who would save the world. We who came from the dust of the earth.

Love is the most powerful fruit of the Spirit, Gal. 5:22;
Love is the most powerful spiritual weapon, Jude 1:21;
Why? Because **GOD IS LOVE**, I John 4:16, and *Love* never fails, I Corinthians 13:8

The Lord Demonstrates the Depths of His Love for Us in John 3:16-17,

For God so greatly loved *and* dearly prized the world that He [even] gave up His only begotten (unique) Son, so that whoever believes in (trusts in, clings to, relies on) Him shall not perish (come to destruction, be lost) but have eternal (everlasting) life. For God did not send the Son into the world in order to judge (to reject, to condemn, to pass sentence on) the world, but that the world might find salvation *and* be made safe *and* sound through Him.

Jesus is able to love beyond human comprehension as He laid His life down for others. In addition to being obedient to Father God, He had a very deep love. "…for the Lord sees not as man sees; for man looks on the outward appearance, but the Lord looks on the heart," I Sam. 16:7.

He has great compassion for people and understands their weaknesses and bondages. Yet he was determined to see them set free and to live in His liberty, freedom and the abundant life He was sent to achieve through His sacrifice and obedience to the Father.

Jesus was also grateful in His heart and very thankful for what was entrusted to Him. Father God could trust Him for He only did and said what He was sent to do by Father God in heaven. *As a result, many benefited from His love, sacrifice, obedience and compassion as miracles (the supernatural) went forth for others.*

His love surpasses all understanding. He is a gift from Heaven to all who will receive Him as their personal Savior and Lord. His disciples and followers are known today as Believers who are trained, equipped and sent to those who are lost and hurting in various areas of their lives.

Believers are anointed and sent by those today that have the same authority as the Lord used when He sent His twelve disciples out.

In Matthew 10:1 it says,

> And Jesus summoned to Him His twelve disciples and gave them power *and* authority over unclean spirits, to drive them out, and to cure all kinds of disease and all kinds of weakness and infirmity."

When Jesus' disciples were saved (born-again) and filled with the infilling of Holy Spirit with the evidence of speaking in an unknown tongue which began on the day of Pentecost (Acts 2:1-4; I Cor. 14:2) they went about ministering the Gospel. They prayed, shared God's heart and laid hands on the sick with compassion and boldness then signs and wonders followed, Acts 4:29-30.

Many people say they want to be like Jesus but in to be like Him you must be ready to love others with an unconditional love. To be willing to lay hands on the sick, be available to pray for others, to do for others, to cast out demons from others and help them be set free from oppression or possession.

These acts should start first with your own family since your family is your first ministry if you are a Believer. All Christians are ministers and called to speak the Gospel, the Good News about the Kingdom of God. Tell others it is available for all those who believe and receive salvation. Others include neighbors, friends, co-workers, strangers and anyone you are led to share the Good News with.

The Holy Spirit will guide you and place people across your path to speak with. Or in some cases, your life can be an example as God ministers and intervenes for others. However done, know it is not something to be pressured by. You may even find people approaching you as they have prayed and are led to receive answers they seek as God uses you as His mouthpiece and your hands as instruments for healing. These are just a few reasons why it is important to spend time with God in prayer and worship as well as in study. Being sensitive to Him makes it easier to be directed by His leading.

Jesus' disciples, those in the Kingdom of God, should be willing to express their love back to their heavenly Father and His beloved Son. In addition, expressing God's love to others. They need to love themselves in a healthy way as they follow His instructions and do as He stated in the greatest command given to mankind.

Matthew 22:37-40 Gives us the Greatest Command Ever,

> And He replied to him, You shall love the Lord your God with all your heart and with all your soul and with all your mind (intellect). This is the great (most important, principal) and first commandment. And a second is like it: You shall love your neighbor as [you do] yourself. These two commandments sum up *and* upon them depend all the Law and the Prophets.

The Greatest Commandment was fulfilled with Love. All the Law and the Prophets hang on these two commandments because these two instructions fulfill the Law, Matthew 22:37-40. Love covers sin and love heals. When we truly love others, we will not desire to do anything that will hurt or harm them. We will choose to walk upright before God, Who is Love. John 14:15 tells us, "If you [really] love Me, you will keep (obey) My commands." His commandments are loving instructions given to enable and empower His people to live a successful and fruitful life.

The most profound expression of His love for us is the gift of His only Son, prepared and sent to be our Savior and Lord. *Our receiving His Gift of Love will be the greatest decision we will ever make.*

God Declares He is Love and there is No Greater Love than His

While We Were Still Sinners, Christ Died for Us, Romans 5:6-8 says,

> While we were yet in weakness [powerless to help ourselves], at the fitting time Christ died for (in behalf of) the ungodly. Now it is an extraordinary thing for one to give his life even for an upright man, though perhaps for a noble

and lovable *and* generous benefactor someone might even dare to die. But God shows *and* clearly proves His [own] love for us by the fact that while we were still sinners, Christ (the Messiah, the Anointed One) died for us.

Your Sin Not Counted Against You, Romans 4:7-8 NIV says,

"Blessed are those whose transgressions are forgiven, whose sins are covered. Blessed is the one whose sin the Lord will never count against them."

I John 4:7-16 NIV says,

Dear friends, let us love one another, for love comes from God. Everyone who loves has been born of God and knows God. Whoever does not love does not know God, because God is love. This is how God showed his love among us: He sent his one and *only Son into the world that we might live through him. This is love*: not that we loved God, but ***that he loved us and sent his Son as an atoning sacrifice for our sins.*** Dear friends, since God so loved us, we also ought to love one another. No one has ever seen God; but if we love one another, God lives in us and his love is made complete in us. This is how we know that we live in him and he in us: He has given us his Spirit. And we have seen and testify that the Father has sent his Son to be the Savior of the world. If anyone acknowledges that Jesus is the Son of God, God lives in them and they in God. And so we know and rely on the love God has for us. *God is love. Whoever lives in love lives in God, and God in them.* (Emphasis added.)

When we make the choice to yield to the ways of God then it says, "For I will be merciful and gracious toward their sins and *I will remember their deeds of unrighteousness no more,"* Heb. 8:12. In another passage it is written, *"And their sins and their lawbreaking I will remember no more,"* Heb. 10:17. And in another it says, "...*For I will forgive their iniquity, and I will [seriously] remember their sin no more,"* Jer. 31:34.

His ways are not our ways; God will give instant forgiveness, show mercy, restore and remove from His mind any and all sin you have committed. In return He asks us to make a conscious decision not to sin against Him. And if we sin know that He has already paid the price and given us a way of escape and has never stopped loving us no matter what state we were in.

Although keep in mind, He expects us to grow and mature in our relationship with Him as we learn the things of the Spirit as we are taught by our Comforter and by studying His Word to increase in the knowledge of Who He is. Then our sin nature will decrease and weaken because of the renewing of our minds according to, Romans 12:2.

When you feel uneasy *in your heart* (your spirit) about doing something and then decide to ignore it and do it anyway and what you did turns out to be sinful, notice your spirit man was warning you something was wrong and you were about to make the wrong decision. We could learn from this type of experience and be sensitive the next time we feel uneasy and choose not to yield and wait until we sense a peace about what it is we are about to do and if we do not get that "peace" then let it go.

Whether it is for ourselves or for the benefit of being an example at that moment for someone else, whenever we decide not to trust and rest in God we are more than likely going to do things that would later cause condemnation which is used by the enemy to weaken our faith and to bring guilt.

Responding to and Receiving His Love

We are to love as He loves and live as He lives. The greatest demonstration of the Love God gave us will cause us to be whole. His love has made it possible for us to have a peaceful, prosperous, blessed and sound lifestyle. In other words, a lifestyle that is whole with nothing missing and nothing broken.

Though we will experience opposition because mankind has a spiritual enemy who works through deceived and/or evil people to accomplish his goals. We as people of God can still have what God promised. As we make a decision to receive the higher lifestyle doing things His way, this and only this will ensure we receive all He has for us.

Our peaceful life can be obtained when we keep our minds on Him, I Cor. 2:16. Also, as we remember Jesus is the Prince of Peace (Sar Shalom) who said, "Peace I leave with you; My [own] peace I now give *and* bequeath to you. Not as the world gives do I give to you. Do not let your hearts be troubled, neither let them be afraid, [Stop allowing yourselves to be agitated and disturbed; and do not permit yourselves to be fearful and intimidated and cowardly and unsettled.]," John 14:27.

When we keep God first in our life and when we follow His instructions from His Holy Scriptures, everything He tells us or warns us of is for our good because of the *love in His heart for His creation* and His desire to fellowship and be a part of our lives.

His prosperity includes His love. His prosperity is not limited like the world's prosperity. His includes being prosperous in every area of your life. In your relationships, family (Gen. 12:3); health (3 John 2); finances (Deut. 8:18); spiritual gifts (I Cor. 12:7-11); and talents. Prosperous in joy and beautiful things that are the desires of your heart.

You will be blessed. Blessed not only to enjoy your life but also to be able to bless someone else.

Blessing others is an expression of love. When you truly love others, it is truly unconditional and you have a joy in watching them prosper. (See *God's Way and Finances* for additional information regarding prosperity and other financial information that will bring you into a state of wholeness in God's Kingdom economy.)

According to His Word How are We to Love?

Jesus taught, we are to love everyone, including our enemies! As He sees it, all people were created in God's image. He is no respecter of persons and rather we not be as well. He looks upon the hearts and would desire we do the same and stop judging one another by outer appearance. Have compassion for your fellowman and try to get along with everyone, if at all possible. Jesus practiced what He preached! Let us try to do the same.

Luke 10:27 says, "… You must love the Lord your God with all your heart and with all your soul and with all your strength and with all your mind; and your neighbor as yourself."

John 14:15 says, "If you [really] love Me, you will keep (obey) My commands."

I John 4:19-20 says, "We love *Him* because He first loved us. If anyone says, I love God, and hates (detests, abominates) his brother [in Christ], he is a liar; for he who does not love his brother, whom he has seen, cannot love God, Whom he has not seen."

John 13:34 says, "I give you a new commandment: that you should love one another. Just as I have loved you, so you too should love one another.

His Love and Compassion Actually Offends Some People

When they were offended it was because they could not see or hear what the Spirit of God was saying or understanding what He was doing. Therefore, the spirit on or around them was offended. Some belong to another spirit and did not choose for the greater Spirit, the Holy Spirit, to dwell in and with them.

Signs and wonders follow those who believe Mark 16:17. "When Jesus went ashore and saw a great throng (crowd) of people, *He had compassion* (pity and deep sympathy) for them and cured their sick," Mt.14:14. His compassion for others was major in releasing the anointing that healed the sick and for other miracles Holy Spirit did through Him.

When these signs and wonders followed Jesus' ministry there were those who were offended by it and opposed it greatly.

The expression of love actually caused those who were "spiritually blind" (I Cor. 2:14) to hate instead of love and not to be excited and happy that people were being set free from long term illnesses and bondages. They hate both the Father and the Son of God for the good they have done and continue to do.

John 15:23-25 Talks about the Hatred from Others,

> Whoever hates Me also hates My Father. If I had not done (accomplished) among them the works which no one else ever did, they would not be guilty of sin. But [the fact is] now they have both seen [these works] and have hated both Me and My Father. But [this is so] that the word written in their Law might be fulfilled, **They hated Me without a cause.** (Emphasis added.)

Jesus Comments about Hatred, John 15:18,

> If the world hates you, know that it hated Me before it hated you.

The God of this World has Blinded Some, 2 Cor. 4:4,

> For the god of this world has blinded the unbelievers' minds [that they should not discern the truth], preventing them from

seeing the illuminating light of the Gospel of the glory of Christ (the Messiah), Who is the image *and* likeness of God. (Also see John 8:44.)

Our Understanding of His Love

We understand that *one of God's greatest gifts of love is to impart divine wisdom.* A higher wisdom, the knowledge of the divine plan previously hidden that is not of this present age and a great deal more than what the world offers.

He invites us to draw near to Him and in doing so stay connected to the Living Word that will give us the wisdom we need, James 4:8. As we stay connected to Him, He will reveal mysteries we can keep forever, Deut. 29:29. Those mysteries will benefit not only our lives but our children and those around us.

Spiritual Wisdom Comes from Living Words, I Cor. 2:6-12, 16, NKJV

However, we speak wisdom among those who are mature, yet not the wisdom of this age, nor of the rulers of this age… But we speak the wisdom of God in a mystery, the hidden *wisdom* which God ordained before the ages for our glory…

"Eye has not seen, nor ear heard, Nor have entered into the heart of man The

things which God has prepared for those who love Him. "

But God has revealed *them* to us through His Spirit. For the Spirit searches all things, yes, the deep things of God... no one knows the things of God except the Spirit of God. Now we have received, not the spirit of the world, but the Spirit who is from God, that we might know the things that have been freely given to us by God.

For *"who has known the mind of the LORD that he may instruct Him?"* But *we have the mind of Christ.*

As we follow His instructions and will (His plans and purpose) throughout His Word, we will reap the benefits and rewards that go beyond our dreams and what we can imagine, Eph. 3:20. We will surely receive divine wisdom which will protect the destiny God has for us.

True Compassion for God and People Grows out of God's Love

Three main components will remain with the family of God throughout eternity.

I Corinthians 13:13 NIV Reveals what they are,

And now these *three remain*: faith, hope and love. **But the greatest of these is love.** (Emphasis added.)

Jesus has great compassion for people and was grateful in His heart and very thankful. He only did and said what He was sent to do and as a result many benefited from His obedience and miracles (the supernatural) went forth in great measure. As mentioned earlier He dealt with the demonic realm, casting demons out of people and setting them free.

The most profound expression of the love of God is the gift of His only Beloved Son. **It is love that seeks the best interest of an individual while seeking nothing for itself in return**. God's purpose was to save over judgment or condemnation and for this reason God is declared to be "Love," I John 4:8, 16.

As we follow His example and choose to love without expecting anything in return, our marriages, families and friendships will blossom beyond our expectations because there should not be any selfish motive attached. Sincerity will shine and true healing of the heart will come forth.

Illustrations and Nuggets of God's Love

Without love, nothing will be long term in your life because God is Love and apart from Him you can do nothing, John 15:5. God said in His Word without faith we cannot please Him but yet it is love that activates our faith. We cannot use our faith to its greatest potential if we are not giving and receiving the love of God.

Love is a major key in having success in all relationships. When you walk or live a life of love, you are walking with God, *to walk with God is to stay in step with His Holy Spirit*.

According to I Peter 1:22, the Holy Spirit is the One who purifies our hearts so the *pure sincere love of God can flow through us* and out to others. "As we allow the love of God to work or flow through us, it will enable us to ever be filled with the Holy Spirit. We are to walk as children of Light and be filled with the Spirit because the fruit of the Light or the Spirit [consists] in every form of kindly goodness, uprightness of heart, and trueness of life" Ephesians 5:8-9, paraphrased.

The Law of Love is found in Luke 6:27-31 and it basically *tells us how to express love to those who have come against us*. For example, verse 27 tells us to make it a practice to love our enemies by doing *good* to those who hate us. One of the first things we are to do is to pray for them. When this is done you open a door for God to heal your heart because of your obedience to a spiritual principle and command. And in Luke 6:31 (NAS), the Golden Rule says, "And just as you want people to treat you, treat them in the same way." When we choose to obey God, we free ourselves up from bondage to whatever or whomever.

As you *choose love over bitterness,* strife or some other demonic spirit, you will have the victory every time. *When love is expressed* through kindness, thoughtfulness, forgiveness, respect, humility, self-control, honor, gentleness, goodness, peace, patience, faithfulness, caring actions and deeds, you are then walking in His love and thereby abiding in Him. This will open the door for God to turn things around. His ways are not our ways, they are higher, Isaiah 55:8-9.

We can avoid many negative things from coming into our lives if we would just *humble ourselves and follow His spiritual instructions.* They may not make sense to the natural mind, but if done, it will cause things to turn around for our good. One example of an instruction or command that makes absolutely no sense to the natural mind (I Corinthians 2:14) is to forgive those who have wronged you. Perhaps we have not considered, the Lord has forgiven us of *all our failings and shortcomings* and He desires we follow His example and do the same toward others, Mark 11:25-26.

If you follow through and do what He has asked, even though it does not make any sense to you, you will find, because of *a step of faith,* it works. It *will allow you to receive a supernatural healing from a Supernatural God.* Healing in any area of your life where it is needed is connected to your being able to forgive others.

That in turn will close doors that were opened because of unforgiveness which if not dealt with can cause a root of bitterness. When a root of bitterness occurs, every evil practice can be released. Bitterness opens a door to the enemy then he has access to attack you. You created a place for the adversary to work when you shut God and His ways out. To shut the door on the enemy, repent from your heart, receive forgiveness, speak to God receive new instructions and continue forward.

Guard love and take care of it, because it is the most valuable tool or spiritual weapon you will ever have. There is no weapon formed against love that will *ever* be able to stand.

Great Characteristics of *True or Mature Love* are Found in the Love Chapter, I Corinthians 13:4-8 in "The Book,"

> Love is very patient and kind, never jealous or envious, never boastful or proud, never haughty or selfish or rude. Love does not demand its own way. It is not irritable or touchy. It does not hold grudges and will hardly even notice when others do it wrong. It is never glad about injustice, but rejoices *whenever* truth wins out. If you love someone you will be loyal to him no matter what the cost. You will always believe in him, always expect the best of him, and always stand your ground in defending him.

I Corinthians 13:7-8 in the Amplified Bible is Equally as Powerful Regarding Love,

> Love bears up under anything and everything that comes, is ever ready to believe the best of every person, its hopes are fadeless under all circumstances, and it endures everything [without weakening]. Love never fails...

The Love Chapter describes God's idea of mature love. Notice what is included: patience, kindness, being joyful with truth, trust, loyalty, full of hope and enduring or totally committed. Unconditional love will allow you to communicate correctly, having the right attitude with your husband or wife or children and others while allowing God to work on any changes that need to be done with all persons involved including yourself.

If your goal or motive is to really show someone else love, then you should remember *if it is not unconditional love then it really is not love at all.* If it is a "heart" issue, only God can change and/or heal a human heart and cause it to align with His will.

And may the Lord make you to increase and excel and overflow in love for one another and for all people, just as we also do for you,
I Thessalonians 3:12
(Emphasis added.)

Chapter 6

His Kingdom, Kingship and Royal Power

"For to us a Child is born, to us a Son is given; and the *government* shall be upon His shoulder…" Isaiah 9:6.

His Kingdom (Government) is Not of This World!

"His Kingdom is not of this world, His was not a physical kingdom based on war and violence. **His is a Spiritual Kingdom establishing the truth in the world**. Being part of His Kingdom is knowing God, who is Truth, and whom we know as we know Jesus," [1] John 18:33-37; 1 John 2:3.

John 18:36-37 Confirms His is a Kingdom of Truth,

Jesus answered, My Kingdom (kingship, royal power) belongs not to this world. If My kingdom were of this world, My followers would have been fighting to keep Me… But as it is, My kingdom is not from here (this world); [it has no such origin or source].

Pilate said to Him, Then You are a King? Jesus answered, You say it! [You speak correctly!] For I am a King. [Certainly I am a King!] This is why I was born, and for this I have come into the world, to bear witness to the Truth. Everyone who is of the Truth [who is a friend of the Truth, who belongs to the Truth] hears *and* listens to My voice.

God's Governmental Structure on the Earth

The Fivefold Government Structure Set-Up by the Messiah, Eph. 4:11-13,

And His gifts were [varied; He Himself appointed and gave men to us] some to be apostles (special messengers), some prophets (inspired preachers and expounders), some evangelists (preachers of the Gospel, traveling missionaries), some pastors (shepherds of His flock) and teachers.

His intention was the perfecting *and* the full equipping of the saints (His consecrated people), [that they should do] the work of ministering toward building up Christ's body (the church),

[That it might develop] until we all attain oneness in the faith and in the comprehension of the [full and accurate] knowledge of the Son of God, that [we might arrive] at really mature manhood (the completeness of personality which is nothing less than the standard height of Christ's own perfection), the measure of the stature of the fullness of the Christ *and* the completeness found in Him.

His Kingdom is Open and Welcomes Everyone Jew and Gentile

One of the reasons it was significant for Jesus' (Yeshua) birth to take place in Bethlehem is it was the original home of Naomi and the dwelling place of Ruth the Moab woman who became a part of Israel when she declared to Naomi "...*Your people shall be my people and your God my God...* and they came to Bethlehem," Ruth 1:16-19.

This relates to the nations, the Gentiles, coming to know the True God of Israel by embracing Yeshua/Jesus as their Lord and Savior. In Isaiah 42:6 it says the *Messiah would be a light to the nations (the Gentiles) and give them a covenant.* The heart of Ruth was grateful she had come to know the God of Israel, this represented grafting in of the Gentiles into the family of God and becoming the "One New Man." (Romans 11:17-19; Eph. 2:14-20; I Cor. 12:12-13.)

Her life is a demonstration of an attitude to bless the people who brought us the Messiah which by the way came through one of her descendants after she married Boaz and had a child named Obed who was the grandfather of King David, Matthew 1:5-6. This demonstrated God honored her for honoring her Jewish mother-in-law and *God blessed her life when she herself honored the God of Israel*.

Kingship and Other Offices of the Messiah

Another reason for Jesus being born in Bethlehem was the fact King David was also born there as well as anointed there by the Prophet Samuel to be Saul's successor. Jesus was called the *Son of David* (Isaiah 9:6-7) which is an important part of His identity as the Jewish Messiah as shown in Matthew 21:9 where the Jewish crowds welcomed Him as *Hosanna in the Highest*.

Jesus Confirms He is a King, John 18:37 NKJV,

Pilate said to Him, Then You are a King? Jesus answered, You say it! [You speak correctly!] For I am a King. [Certainly I am a King!] This is why I was born, and for this I have come into the world, to bear witness to the Truth. Everyone who is of the Truth [who is a friend of the Truth, who belongs to the Truth] hears *and* listens to My voice.

He is the promised "Seed" of the woman that shall bruise the head of Satan, Genesis 3:15; Gal. 4:4. Through King David's offspring (Seed) his throne shall be established forever, 2 Sam. 7:16-17. As long as the sun and the moon exist he will have a throne. God swore by His holiness this would be done because of the covenant He made with David.

David's Throne will Exist as Long as there is a Sun and a Moon, Psalms 89:35-37 NKJV declares,

Once I have sworn by My holiness; I will not lie to David: His seed shall endure forever, And his throne as the sun before Me; It shall be established forever like the moon, Even *like* the faithful witness in the sky.

Yeshua's assignment or mission as a *perfect man* who never sinned was the *Redeemer of the lost* (those without a covenant with God). While on the earth, the Messiah functioned in various offices as He was a blessing to others.

He was an ***Orthodox Jewish Rabbi, a Master Teacher*** in the Synagogues where He imparted great wisdom and healing, Matthew 22:16 and John 3:2 NKJV which says, "This man came to Jesus by night and said to Him, "Rabbi, we know that You are a teacher come from God; for no one can do these signs that You do unless God is with him." Additional passages, Matthew 4:23; Matthew 21:23; John 13:13 and many more demonstrated He was a Teacher.

He also functioned in the office of an ***Apostle,*** Isa. 61:1 One who is sent; and as a ***Prophet of God,*** John 4:42-44; Matthew 13:57 and Matthew 21:11. As a ***High Priest,*** Heb.4:14-16; as a ***Preacher,*** Eph.2:17; Isa. 61:1; and as a ***King,*** 2 Sam.7:16-17; Ps. 89:29-37; John 18:37.

In Jesus We Are the One New Man

If you consider yourself to be a part of the Family of God because of the Finished Work the Messiah did at the Cross it means you have declared you are a part of the "One New Man." God desires Jews and Gentiles come together in Messiah and worship as One New Man in faith.

The two groups which worshipped together and operated in the fivefold ministry gifts (Eph. 4:11-16) in the early church during the first century witnessed many miracles, power and blessings because of coming together in Yeshua HaMashiach/Jesus the Christ. The two groups were separated during the Dark Ages or the Medieval Times and it was never God's will, plan or desire for them to do so.

We are called and destined to be one in the Kingdom of God, worshipping the One True Living God! There are benefits for both the Jewish Believer and the Non-Jewish Believer. As we continue moving forward insight, fresh revelation and understanding of the old covenant of **what was concealed,** to the understanding and revelation of **what is being revealed** in the new covenant will change and advance God's Kingdom and give us life to the full as He purposed, John 10:10.

The Old and New Covenants are respectfully known as the Holy Bible. The New Testament in Hebrew is known as the Tanakh. The first five books are referred to as the Torah. The New Testament in Hebrew is called B'rit Hadashah.

As we draw neigh to God, He will draw neigh to us, James 4:8. As One New Man we will continue forward in Jesus' name and restore what was stolen from God's people. We decree insight, understanding, revelation, miracles, the fivefold ministry gifts and the gifts of the Spirit, I Cor. 12:7-11, 28 will be utilized in Believers as God wills. We will operate in faith, spiritual gifts, talents with signs and wonders to such a degree God's glory will manifest on the earth like we have never seen before.

We decree the structure of the fivefold ministry (Eph. 4:11-16) that was stolen from *the church will be restored during this new church age through the One New Man.* The Kingdom of God in turn will continue to advance to the Glory of the King of kings. *It is His hour and time to reveal His Glory,* restore, recover and make new. It is Jubilee and harvest time for those who can believe!

Furthermore, as a One New Man in the Kingdom of God you would be referred to as a Christian or as a Messianic Jew; as a Believer; as Born-again; a Saint; an Evangelical; a Child of God; Saved; a son or daughter of God; a child of God; and as a sister or brother in the Lord to name a few terms used in the Kingdom of God regarding your choice to having received the Messiah Jesus/Yeshua as your Lord and Savior. But before the word Christianity was used the first Believers who were Jewish followers in the Messiah, the Anointed One of Israel were His church and it was called "The Way!"

Ephesians 2:12-20 says,

> [Remember] that you were at that time separated (living apart) from Christ [excluded from all part in Him], utterly estranged and outlawed from the rights of Israel as a nation, and strangers with no share in the sacred compacts of the [Messianic] promise [with no knowledge of or right in God's agreements, His covenants]. *And you had no hope (no promise); you were in the world without God. But now in Christ Jesus, you who*

once were [so] far away, through (by, in) the blood of Christ have been brought near. For He is [Himself] our peace (our bond of unity and harmony). ***He has made us both [Jew and Gentile] one [body], and has broken down (destroyed, abolished) the hostile dividing wall between us,*** by abolishing in His [own crucified] flesh the enmity [caused by] the Law with its decrees and ordinances [which He annulled]; that He from the two might create in Himself **ONE NEW MAN** [one new quality of humanity out of the two], so making peace. And *[He designed] to reconcile to God both [Jew and Gentile, united] in a single body by means of His cross, thereby killing the mutual enmity and bringing the feud to an end.* And He came and preached the glad tidings of peace to you who were afar off and [peace] to those who were near. For it is through Him that we both [whether far off or near] now have an introduction (access) by one [Holy] Spirit to the Father [so that we are able to approach Him]. Therefore, you are no longer outsiders (exiles, migrants, and aliens, excluded from the rights of citizens), but you now share citizenship with the saints (God's own people, consecrated and set apart for Himself); and you belong to God's [own] household. You are built upon the foundation of the apostles and prophets with Christ Jesus Himself the chief Cornerstone. (Emphasis added.)

"Christ destroyed the division between Jews and non-Jews, providing all people the opportunity to be saved by grace. In His death He reconciled sinners to God, destroying our hatred for Him. Thus Jesus/Yeshua opened the way for us to live in God's presence. The Holy Spirit is that presence of God with us. Jesus founded the church and is the uniting power for it" [2] Ephesians 2:14-22.

The Kingdom of God Mindset vs. Other Mindsets

There are three different major types of mindsets in the earth today and they are as follows: (1) The Kingdom of God's Mindset is the Hebrew, Hebraic or Biblical Mindset; (2) The Greek Mindset; and (3) The Barbarian or Barbaric Mindset. Many individuals will function a great deal in one type of mindset and maybe a portion in another.

The Hebrew Biblical Mindset

The goal is to function or operate with the mind of the True and Living God. The God of Abraham, Isaac and Jacob and acquire the mind of Christ, I Cor. 2:16.

The Hebraic Mindset is spiritual. The Hebraic mindset will show you how to operate in the spiritual realm. You are working with Words that are full of spirit and life. The Word of God is God (John 1:1) and will work for you if you are focusing on keeping God first.

You can begin with a prayer. Just as a point of contact, touch your head and heart and pray for your brain and mind. Ask God to change your brain and your mind (heart) to operate and work by His divine designed plan.

Prayer is important for everyone especially those Born-again (saved) who have the mind of Christ developing from the moment they receive salvation. Once your salvation is received your spirit man receives God's Holy Spirit and begins working in, for and through you. Your Christlike thinking will develop as you walk by faith (trust).

A key way to develop a Hebrew Biblical Mindset is to meditate on the Word, God's Holy Bible. Think on it over and over, ponder it day and night, Psalm 1:1-3. You are filling your brain and heart (mind) with the thoughts of God. This will also lead to transforming your mind, Romans 12:2.

The enemy (adversary) uses oppression and other devices to try and hinder the work God has for your life. The enemy will send thoughts of doubt, fear and unbelief that speak to your mind to try to get you off track (out of the cycle of life and timing of God).

To halt the attacks on your mind from the adversary guard your mind by guarding what you think on. If thoughts are depressing, self-destructive and harmful take them captive, rebuke them and cast down any negative thoughts, 2 Cor. 10:4-5. Then think on purpose the higher things God as instructed all of us to think on, Phil. 4:8-9.

You can also pray in your heavenly language to change your focus, I Cor. 14:2. If you do not have your heavenly language then rebuke the thoughts. Also, repent when necessary for old mindsets. Allow God to give you His mindset and receive a fresh start as you move forward with the right mind frame.

God Almighty gave the Hebrew language to His chosen people to communicate with Him and with one another. And the assignment to write the holy scriptures were given to Jewish prophets as they wrote under the inspiration of Holy Spirit. God's Hebraic Mindset is represented in the Holy Bible which is the Word of God. His Word tells us His thoughts and ways are not ours they are higher, Isaiah 55:8-9.

When you begin to think like God does, your thoughts will align with His and not only will your life change because of the transforming of your mind (Romans 12:2) but you will prosper, 3 John 2. You will prosper in every area of your life including your peace, relationships, finances, health and so forth. You will also gain a new perspective on life.

In addition, you will receive divine wisdom, clarity in your thoughts and divine favor. You will become more sensitive to Holy Spirit making it easier to receive from God's Spirit, direction, instructions, guidance, strategies and much more. As you communicate and fellowship with the Lord, voids in your life will be filled in your soul (mind, will and emotions).

As you operate in society today with a Biblical Mindset based on the Word of God things will be accomplished God's way and calculates to success for you. We learn how to live within the boundaries set for us that keep us safe and give us protection.

The Biblical Mindset will seem foolish to those who are not Born-again because they function with a different mindset. Those Born-again (saved) have been grafted (adopted) into the Family of God with the New Covenant Messiah gave to His people that was spoken in, Jeremiah 31:31-33 and in Hebrews 8:7-12.

I Cor. 2:14-16 NKJV Demonstrates How the World Views a Godly Mindset. Worldly People are Spiritually Blind to Truth,

But the natural man does not receive the things of the Spirit of God, for they are foolishness to him; nor can he know *them,* because they are spiritually discerned. But he who is spiritual judges all things, yet he himself is *rightly* Judged by no one. For *"who has known the mind of the LORD* that he may instruct Him?" But we have the mind of Christ.

One example is found in Jeremiah 38:14-15 where Zedekiah king of Judah sent for Jeremiah the prophet and asked him a question and instructed him not to hold anything back. "Jeremiah said to Zedekiah, "If I give you an answer, will you not kill me? Even if I did give you counsel, you would not listen to me."

This is the situation. The king, a worldly man (a person without a covenant with God) sent for the prophet of God for clarity and/or instructions.

But because the Hebrew Mindset of God is different from the Greek and Barbaric Mindsets the person that is not of God will not understand the spiritual aspect. God will not do things the way man does them, His ways are greater and higher. They may even sound foolish to the average mind.

The Worldly Perception of the Biblical Mindset, I Cor. 2:14,

> But the natural, nonspiritual man does not accept *or* welcome *or* admit into his heart the gifts *and* teachings *and* revelations of the Spirit of God, for they are folly (meaningless nonsense) to him; and he is incapable of knowing them [of progressively recognizing, understanding, and becoming better acquainted with them] because they are spiritually discerned *and* estimated *and* appreciated.

In this meeting Jeremiah gave the king specific instructions to follow that would have saved his kingdom and family from the king of Babylon.

However, because king Zedekiah did not agree with the prophetic word or he was afraid for a lack of faith, he did not follow through with the instructions and what the prophet said came to pass, Jeremiah 38. The king lost his throne, his sons and all the nobles of Judah were murdered in front of him and then his eyes were put out. He was also bound and taken to Babylon. The Babylonians set fire to the royal palace and the houses of the people, Jeremiah 39.

This could have been avoided had the king listened to the prophet of God. Today God is still speaking and giving edification, encouragement, instructions, comfort and warnings, I Cor. 14:3. God can speak through His prophets or anyone or any way He chooses. The Bible says in 2 Chron. 20:20, "…Believe in the Lord your God and you shall be established; believe *and* remain steadfast to His prophets and you shall prosper."

But because people do not understand the mind of YHVH (Messiah), they choose to ignore Him and take matters in their own hands with their own strength and consequently fail. In the book of Zech. 4:6 NKJV it says, it won't be in our strength or power but His, "…Not by might nor by power, but by My Spirit, says the LORD of hosts."

The Greek Mindset

The Greek Mindset came into being after the "Reformation initiated by Martin Luther happened at the same time as the Renaissance when Europe was changing from Barbarian back to Greek thinking. So, at the time of the Reformation, the church embraced the Greek mindset."

The Greek mindset is about knowledge and what you can accomplish on your own not so much leaning on God but putting themselves first and taking charge of their own lives.

When you think you are intelligent enough or strong enough in your mind to overcome most obstacles in your life, to reach the destiny you desire and you think you don't need God, you have a Greek Mindset. This mindset leans on your own understanding not willing to lean on and follow God because you cannot figure out everything He tells you to do.

Repent and learn to walk and follow the Holy Spirit who will always lead you to operate in a Hebraic mindset.

The Greek mindset in the church was very dangerous because leaders and layman will try to apply logic and reasoning to interpret the Scriptures. This will only lead to trying to figure God out. Trying to get every point of doctrine in the Bible right according to what you think is correct because you thought you were smart enough to figure God out. Not realizing you are being deceived.

Even today the people of God are still in bondage to political and religious systems set in place during the Dark Ages. They can be changed with the Hebraic mindset securing God's way without wavering, doubting, as we move into the cycles of life and blessings God has provided.

We must come up over the Greek mindset. Ask Sincerely for the King of Glory to come into your life. Desire the Living Word to align and connect with God and take on His character and attributes more and more.

The Barbarian Mindset

Dominate, intimidate to move forward and/or to control others. One is taught in different ways either you agree with me, my system, my interest, or my way of doing things or you will be tortured or killed.

Some people are held captive by this type of mindset when they think they must dominate and intimidate others to progress in life. Not realizing as they try to hold or hinder someone else back or to instill fear in them, they are only planting seed that the same thing is done to them by someone sent that is worse than they. We reap what we sow in this life. If you judge you will be judged and so on, Matthew 7.1.

In addition, with a Barbarian Mindset you cannot see a loving God but more than likely a tyrant you must fear. You will also be prone and live in legalism trying to run your life by a lot of rules, regulations and traditions.

Most of the time living in guilt and condemnation because you cannot meet these expectations. There is no mercy or forgiveness everything is cut and dry, black and white. No chances, no forgiveness, no love to bring healing and strength and wholeness.

The Barbarian Mindset is not of the Living God. Living in fear and allowing it to control your life, expecting crisis after crisis to occur in your life is all part of a Barbarian Mindset. The Lord does not want this for your life and you block Him out and /or hinder Him from working for you.

To be set free, simply with a sincere heart, repent for living outside of God's Word and best for you. Repent for living in fear and for anything you did to instill fear in others.

Desiring the Kingdom of God and its Benefits

God is a Spirit, John 4:24. He lives in the Spiritual realm which is more real than the physical realm we see with our physical eyes. Everything was created out of His Spirit. That means everything came forth from the spiritual realm first and manifested in the physical, Genesis 1:1-31. Therefore, the spiritual realm is more real than the physical.

The Kingdom of God is no different. It exists in heaven and was brought to the earth by Jesus for the citizens in His government. God's Kingdom was established on the earth by the Messiah, Jesus Christ, the Anointed One, for them to have hope and to be able to enjoy an abundant life in the midst of a fallen world, John 10:10; Gen. 3.

This world is not the origin of His Kingdom. All its resources and power are not from the earth, but their origin is Heaven.

"It is inclusive in character embracing the natural and spiritual seeds of Abraham." "It is universal in aspect, it is the subject of New Testament revelation and will be eternal in its duration." All its citizens are well protected. They have excellent benefits and supernatural favor in the earth because of their choice of citizenship.

The Kingdom of God is real, with a real government and a real government and a real King who is the King of kings, Rev. 19:16. His government operates in both heaven and over all the earth.

Because the Kingdom of God is spiritual and has no limit or boundaries it operates in heaven and on earth. Therefore, while on earth we operate through the anointing (His power) coming upon His people.

The Bible Declares what His Kingdom is in Romans 14:17 and the Message Version (MSG)

> [After all] the kingdom of God is not a matter of [getting the] food and drink [one likes], but instead it is **righteousness** (that state which makes a person acceptable to God) and [heart] **peace and joy in the Holy Spirit.** (Emphasis added.)

> God's Kingdom isn't a matter of what you put in your stomach, for goodness' sake. It's what God does with your life as he sets it right, puts it together, and completes it with joy.

In other words, the Kingdom is first spiritual. When functioning properly in and with it, it will manifest great spiritual and tangible benefits that will enable you to live successfully while on this earth.

His Kingdom includes righteousness, doing the right thing according to His will. Jesus provided Believers with righteousness (right standing with God) through our faith in Him. It is a gift from God we receive by faith.

Jesus Provided our Righteousness, 2 Cor. 5:21,

For He made Him who knew no sin *to be* sin for us, that we might become the righteousness of God in Him.

In addition, righteousness is a part of the Armor of God so when we put it on it will help protect and persevere us, Eph. 6:14. "For we do not wrestle against flesh and blood, but against principalities, against powers, against the rulers of the darkness of this age…," Eph. 6:12 NKJV. We must believe as citizens in His Kingdom we share in His authority and can move with His power to over throw bad or undesirable circumstances and receive the victory.

Satan works diligently to separate the Believer from fellowship with God. If we result to using the worlds way to achieve things by lying, cheating or stealing we will not have the peace and joy that was promised in the Kingdom of God.

But, as we realize when we live in the Kingdom of God we control the world around us in whatever territory God has given us to take dominion, to be a witness or example for others. We can come boldly to the throne fellowship, ask for assistance, provision, whatever your need may be, Heb. 4:16.

So, as Believers are faced with a difficult choice and we decide to do the right thing we are operating with His righteousness that is within us and functioning according to His Word.

He tells us in Zechariah 4:6 it is not by our might nor by our power, but by His Spirit that we will pass life's test, achieve goals and finish assignments from the Lord and finish well!

Through His grace by faith we can be at peace and be whole. We can experience His peace which He left for us as we learn to rest in Him and trust He is on His throne, John 14:27. That He is all knowing and all powerful can turn whatever situation we face around for our good. Knowing His Holy Spirit dwells in us and is with us also brings great joy, John 16:7-15.

Doing what is right, not by our standard but by His standard, the Bible is what will give us a supernatural peace and joy. When we have genuine peace even during difficult situations and circumstances it means we are at rest, trusting in God which pleases Him, Heb. 11:6; Num. 14:8.

John 15:5, 7 Says We Can Do Nothing Without Him,

> I am the vine, you *are* the branches. He who abides in Me, and I in him, bears much fruit; for without Me you can do nothing... If you abide in Me, and My words abide in you, you will ask what you desire, and it shall be done for you.

When what we do is done with the right mindset, God's mindset, it will produce life. Life accomplishes things which render fruit, multiplication and justice. Then true peace and joy will follow because you live in the Kingdom.

We are a royal race with dual citizenship. Our King, Jesus Christ is the "Prince (Ruler) of the kings of the earth. To Him Who ever loves us and has once [for all] loosed *and* freed us from our sins by His own blood, And formed us into a kingdom (a royal race), priests to His God and father..." All the citizens of His Kingdom will say, "...unto Him be the glory and the power *and* the majesty and the dominion throughout the ages *and* forever and ever, Amen," Rev. 1:5-6.

We are in heaven with Him while on the earth fulfilling our purpose. We are seated in Heaven with Him.

Eph. 2:5-6 Tells Us to be Seated and Rest in Him,

...He made us alive together in fellowship *and* in union with Christ; [He gave us the very life of Christ Himself, the same new life with which He quickened Him, for] it is by grace (His favor and mercy which you did not deserve) that you are saved delivered from judgement and made partakers of Christ's salvation).

> And He raised us up together with Him
> and made us sit down together [giving us
> joint seating with Him] in the heavenly
> sphere [by virtue of our being] in Christ
> Jesus (the Messiah, the Anointed One).

It is not impossible to be seated with Him in heaven and still be on earth. We were made in His image. Not only in character and heart but in trinity. We also have three parts to our being. In the book of, I Thess. 5:23 it mentions we are spirit, soul and body. Therefore, even though our spirit lives in our body, Christ by His Spirit has seated us with Him.

We are in Him and He by the Spirit of God Who is everywhere at once, is in us. He is in a place of rest and because we are in Him we are in a place of rest (trusting) by faith through His grace (His empowerment).

This is only one of the supernatural benefits of being a child of the King. The bottom line, when we seek the Kingdom of God first everything else we need or desire that is in His will and is for our purpose will be added to us.

Matthew 6:33 Confirms All things will be Added When We Choose to Seek the Kingdom of God First,

> But seek (aim at and strive after) first of
> all His kingdom and His righteousness
> (His way of doing and being right), and

then all these things taken together will be given you besides.

His benefits will cause you to be strengthened, forgiven, healed, be able to conquer problems and restored from destruction. He will also "satisfy your mouth with good things So that your youth is renewed like the eagles." All of these benefits are to those who "keep His covenant, and to those who remember His commandments" (instructions), Psalm 103:2-6, 11, 17-18, NKJV.

Entering the Kingdom and Going Beyond

How does one enter God's Kingdom and function with His government to receive the lifestyle this government offers? They are born in the country. Are we talking about a regular baby's birth? Of course not, we are referring to being Born-again (John 3:1-3) and given eternal life (John 3:16) which is the first and most important step to entering the Kingdom.

A Priority to Living in the Kingdom of God, I Peter 1:3-4,

> Praised (honored, blessed) be the God and Father of our Lord Jesus Christ (the Messiah)! **By His boundless mercy we have been born again** to an ever-living hope through the resurrection of Jesus Christ from the dead,

[Born anew] into an inheritance which is beyond the reach of change *and* decay [imperishable], unsullied and unfading, reserved in heaven for you,
(Emphasis added.)

We come into His Kingdom by deciding to make Jesus the Lord of our life. We come as a little child, innocent and with faith (each person is born with a degree of faith apportioned by God to him, Romans 12:3. In other words, everyone is born with enough faith to make a decision for Jesus (Yeshua) to be their Lord and Savior.

So, we come believing God and taking Him at His Word. He then manifests His Kingdom inside of each one of us by the Anointed One, the Christ. By entering the New Covenant Jesus first established for Israel, (Jeremiah 31:31-33) and knowing He would add to His Kingdom all who desired to come, including the lost Gentiles (the nations), Romans 11:11-21.

Once in the Kingdom we must begin to learn of the King Who governs and rules over His Kingdom. There is a throne in heaven and Jesus/Yeshua is seated on that throne and He reigns. His will is perfect and there is no pain, sorrow, lack or hunger in His Kingdom only perfection.

He desires that we manifest the Kingdom in heaven on this earth. We live in a fallen world where there is sickness, poverty, lack, sorrow, pain and sin. We have those things in the earth because we have an enemy named Satan, the Accuser and Adversary, Rev. 12:10.

However, Jesus came as the Second Adam, redeemed us as the Son of God and taught us we overcame the enemy by the blood of the Lamb (His blood that was shed for us) and by the word of our testimony, Rev. 12:11.

Jesus taught the people how to pray for the Kingdom of God to come to the earth, in the Lord's Prayer, Matthew 6:9-13. He taught about the Kingdom and preached the good news, Matthew 4:17. Apostle Paul spoke boldly about the Kingdom of God, and baptized many in the name of Jesus, Acts 19. Our King proclaimed the Kingdom was at hand, He announced what was near and the life that came with it, Mark 1:14-15.

The Kingdom of God is where we can experience peace beyond understanding, safety, unconditional love, prosperity in every area of our lives (relationships, joy, finances, physical health, spiritual, emotional well-being and so forth). As we develop the fruit of the Spirit in our lives we can experience balance and a great deal of wholeness, Gal. 5:22-23.

In the Kingdom we discover our true identity, and realize we have a spiritual enemy, our adversary, Satan. We are in a spiritual war with him, who desires to destroy us, John 10:10. But we also realize we belong to Almighty God who fights for us and shows us how to resist the enemy and his tactics.

As we move forward toward maturity by seeking Him out in His Word and gaining wisdom, understanding and knowledge we will receive favor and be prosperous in all areas of life. We will see and resist as we stand against opposition from the enemy who will try to stop us. But as we stay focused and persevere knowing we can trust God and His Holy Spirit Who has sealed us and has placed a hedge of protection, by faith we can continue with joy. (See *God's Way and Spiritual Warfare* for further information in this area.)

Governmental Kingdom Assignments

People are not so much interested in government leaders, their positions and titles as they are in, what can their government do for them.

The worldly governments pride themselves on their leaders, departments, weaponry, the way the government is structured and all the regulations, policies and laws that come with it.

God's Kingdom government focus is to share first, what His government kingdom actually has to offer to its citizens (the Believers). Once the people know what the benefits are and can see the results of them they will make it a point to seek out the leadership to know more about them.

God's ways are not of this world but are greater and more effective, His government will announce what its plans and purposes are *first.* For example: When Father God spoke to Moses from the burning bush He *revealed His plan* to free His people, Exo. 3:5-10. He offered freedom for the Israelites to leave Egypt and go to the Promise Land. Moses actually had to ask God His name, so he could tell the people Who sent him, Exodus 3:14.

The following is an example of the Lord giving part of His plan and fulfilling prophecy: Before Jesus/Yeshua arrived, John the Baptist who was carrying the spirit of Elijah the prophet and who in the wilderness baptized "the people of all the country of Judea and all the inhabitants of Jerusalem" as they repented and asked for forgiveness of sins.

He was sent to announce and prepare the way for the Son of God. It is written in Isaiah 40:3 as well as Mark 1:2-3, 8 NKJV, "Behold, I send My messenger before Your face, *Who will prepare Your way before You." "The voice of one crying in the wilderness:* 'Prepare the way of the LORD; *Make His paths straight."'* "I indeed baptized you with water, but He will baptize you with the Holy Spirit."

Another example: Jesus as the Son of God spoke about the Kingdom of God being at hand. He spoke about what the Kingdom of God would do for their lives as He demonstrated the power that came with being in the Kingdom of God.

Jesus told them not to worry about what they would eat or drink or the clothes they would wear if they would first seek the Kingdom of God all other necessities for their lives would be added to them. They should not worry or fret but rest (trust) in Him and all their needs would be taken care of. Plus, there are healings, miracles, peace, joy, abundance and prosperity available in His Kingdom.

Matthew 6:25-33 Tells Us Not to Worry but Trust,

> Therefore I tell you, stop being perpetually uneasy (anxious and worried) about your life, what you shall eat *or what you shall drink;* or about your body, what you shall put on. Is not life greater [in quality] than food, and the body [far above and more excellent] than clothing? Look at the birds of the air…your heavenly Father keeps feeding them. Are you not worth much more than they? … And why should you be anxious about clothes? … But if God so clothes the grass of the field, which today is alive *and* green and tomorrow is tossed into the furnace, will He not much more surely clothe you, O you of little faith?... For the Gentiles (heathen) wish for *and* crave *and* diligently seek all these things, and your heavenly Father knows well that you need them all.

> But seek (aim at and strive after) first of all His kingdom and His righteousness (His way of doing and being right), and then all these things taken together will be given you besides.

If people would seek the Kingdom of God first they will find they must because His instructions will lead them to love Him with all their heart, soul, mind and strength... Mt. 22:37-39. Once you seek Him first, out of obedience, it opens the door to other opportunities and the help you need from Holy Spirit.

Even for property and restoration of family, if you will put Him first He promises it all will be returned. Not only what was put aside by you for a time for His sake, but you shall reap a hundredfold return for all that was lost, Mark 10:29-30.

Jesus the Messiah was always about His Father's business. He told them to seek the Kingdom, the country, His plan first and that would plant seeds of obedience and they would be able to receive all His Kingdom had to offer.

People are interested in a government that will meet their needs with the right kind of protection for its citizens, housing and opportunities of growth and increase.

They could enjoy a lifestyle that gives them freedom, hope, opportunities, second and third chances. A government that is passionate about its beliefs of justice and righteousness for everyone.

Others will inquire about your government when they see what it has done for you. Just as they will inquire about your God when they can see what He has done for you.

People in general are interested in themselves and their family. Therefore, they seek after what will supply their needs, wants and desires. Most seek after money and if money supplies their needs many will make money their god.

As we all know money is only a tool and is a part of the Kingdom of God. It too is released in the abundance when we truly have our hearts and motives in the right place. Seek God first then He will add your hearts desires.

Another point about God's government is it is forever, it will never end. He said He is the First and the Last, the Beginning and the End. Rev. 22:13 says it like this, "I am the Alpha and the Omega, the First and the Last (the Before all and the End of all)."

Since He offers eternity there really is no time associated with Him or His government. Before the beginning *He was* and there is *no End in God.* He always was and He always will be. So, all those with Him will always be as well!

The Lord's Purpose for Government

The Lord's purpose, the original intent or reason His Kingdom was created will prevail and last for eternity.

The Kingdom of God recognizes and acknowledges everyone was born to fulfill a specific call or assignment. In other words, before any person was born into this world there was a specific purpose for their life coming into being.

Part of our purpose is rulership in His government and management of the earth. As we walk in our assignment and purpose we can share the Gospel with others. With Messiah's help we will take back all that was stolen from His people in these End-Times.

The purpose in you is why you were born. God had you in mind for a specific task that needed to be fulfilled in the earth in a certain time frame or period. That is why no one is a mistake. Whatever our purpose is it was thought of before we existed then God created and sent forth each one of us with a destination in life to reach. The people that would ultimately choose Him would be those who will function in His Kingdom on earth.

God's Kingdom will reign forever. He wants to share with His creation, those made in His image and have accepted their call. He is willing to share His love, His government, His rulership, His nature and character, His authority, His power over all the earth and much more. He will rule heaven and allow His government on earth to be ruled by His people. The fact is we will reign with Christ!

Sadly, many never find their purpose let alone complete or accomplish it. The right government can help one find and fulfill their assignment and contribute to making the world a better place for others in their sphere of influence.

All those who believe will reap the rewards and benefits of the Kingdom. They will experience the Kingdom on earth to its fullest.

Jesus' Kingdom of God Responsibilities

Listed below are six primary responsibilities from the Word of God, Jesus Christ / Yeshua HaMashiach is responsible for in His Monarchy. Selections and comments are from Apostle and Bible Prophecy Teacher, Dr. Robert L. Dickey.

1.   Administers the Government of the Kingdom of God

Isaiah 9:6-7 NKJV:
"For unto us a Child is born, Unto us a Son is given; And the government will be upon His shoulder. And His name will be called Wonderful, Counselor, Mighty God, Everlasting Father, Prince of Peace. Of the increase of *His* government and peace *there will be* no end, Upon the throne of David and over His kingdom, To order it and establish it with judgment and justice From that time forward, even forever. The zeal of the Lord of hosts will perform this."

This is the prophecy in the Old Covenant that establishes the fact Christ would have a government and He would be responsible for it. Also, the government would last forever. Finally, He would do it all.

2. Is the Commander of the Army of the Lord

Joshua 5:13-15 NKJV:

"And it came to pass, when Joshua was by Jericho, that he lifted his eyes and looked, and behold, a Man stood opposite him with His sword drawn in His hand. And Joshua went to Him and said to Him, "*Are* You for us or for our adversaries?" So, He said, "No, but *as* Commander of the army of the LORD I have now come." And Joshua fell on his face to the earth and worshiped, and said to Him, "What does my Lord say to His servant?" Then the Commander of the LORD's army said to Joshua, "Take your sandal off your foot, for the place where you stand is holy." And Joshua did so."

Here, Joshua, although he had heard the voice of the Lord, did not discern this was the Lord he was speaking to until the Lord announced that He was the Commander of the army of the Lord. Hearing Who he was facing Joshua fell on his face before the Lord and worshiped Him.

3. Gives the Battle Plan and Marching Orders

Joshua 6:2-5 NKJV:

"And the LORD said to Joshua: "See! I have given Jericho into your hand, its king, *and* the mighty men of valor. You shall march around the city, all you men of war; you shall go all around the city once. This you shall do six days. And seven priests shall bear seven trumpets of rams' horns before the ark.

But the seventh day you shall march around the city seven times, and the priests shall blow the trumpets. It shall come to pass, when they make a long *blast* with the ram's horn, *and* when you hear the sound of the trumpet, that all the people shall shout with a great shout; then the wall of the city will fall down flat. And the people shall go up every man straight before him.""

The Lord now gives Joshua the strategy, plans, methods and the marching orders on how to take the city of Jericho. The instruction to us in the two above scriptures is if we will be attentive and discerning of the Lord He will instruct us as to exactly what we must do to be victorious in battle.

4.   Is the Head of the Church

Ephesians 1:20-23 NKJV:
"which He worked in Christ when He raised Him from the dead and seated *Him* at His right hand in the heavenly *places,* far above all principality and power and might and dominion, and every name that is named, not only in this age but also in that which is to come. And He put all *things* under His feet, and **gave Him to be head over all *things* to the church**, which is His body, the fullness of Him who fills all in all." (Emphasis added.)

This scripture demonstrates how much the Lord treasures those who choose to believe in Him. He considers us as a part of His own body and therefore

He will care for us in that manner. He cared enough for you and me that He personally died for each one of us.

5. Chooses His Commanders

a. Abraham

Genesis 12:1-3 NKJV:
"Now the LORD had said to Abram: "Get out of your country, from your family And from your father's house, To a land that I will show you. I will make you a great nation; I will bless you And make your name great; and you shall be a blessing. I will bless those who bless you, And I will curse him who curses you; And in you all the families of the earth shall be blessed.""

b. Moses

Exodus 3:4, 6, 10 NKJV:
"So when the LORD saw that he turned aside to look, God called to him from the midst of the bush and said, "Moses, Moses!" And he said, "Here I am."

Moreover He said, "I am the God of your father— the God of Abraham, the God of Isaac, and the God of Jacob." And Moses hid his face, for he was afraid to look upon God...

...Therefore, come now, and I will send you to

Pharaoh that you may bring My people, the children of Israel, out of Egypt.""'

c. David

I Samuel 16:12, 13 NKJV:
"So he sent and brought him in. Now he *was* ruddy, with bright eyes, and good-looking. And the LORD said, "Arise, anoint him; for this *is* the one!" Then Samuel took the horn of oil and anointed him in the midst of his brothers; and the Spirit of the LORD came upon David from that day forward. So Samuel arose and went to Ramah.""'

d. The Twelve Apostles

Luke 6:13 NKJV:
"And when it was day, He called His disciples to Himself; and from them He chose twelve whom He also named apostles:"

e. The Apostle Paul

Acts 9:3-6 NKJV:
"As he journeyed he came near Damascus, and suddenly a light shone around him from heaven. Then he fell to the ground, and heard a voice saying to him, "Saul, Saul, why are you persecuting Me?" And he said, "Who are You, Lord?" Then the Lord said, "I am Jesus, whom you are persecuting. It *is* hard for you to kick against the goads." So he, trembling and astonished, said, "Lord, what do You

want me to do?" Then the Lord *said* to him, "Arise and go into the city, and you will be told what you must do.""

f. Chooses Today's Officers and Commanders of His Army

Ephesians 4:11, 12 NKJV:
"And He Himself gave some *to be* apostles, some prophets, some evangelists, and some pastors and teachers, for the equipping of the saints for the work of ministry, for the edifying of the body of Christ,"

Here in a – f, I have presented six cases in which the Lord God, Jesus Christ/Yeshua HaMashiach, chose and/or appointed Believers to lead, command or order the saints (His army) in the battle(s) they were to fight.

6.   Intercedes for His Body (the Church, the Believers/Saints)

Romans 8:34 NKJV:
"Who *is* he who condemns? *It is* Christ who died, and furthermore is also risen, who is even at the right hand of God, who also makes intercession for us."

Just think the **Lord God, our creator**, in the ultimate show of humility would intercede on our behalf to God the Father. Certainly, the Father gave Him all power in Heaven and Earth and that was sufficient to carry out anything He would desire. But He shows us the ultimate combination of *Love, humility and obedience in interceding for us to God the Father*.

Replacement Theology Should Not be A Part of God's Kingdom

One of the devices Satan uses to bring division between Christians and the Jewish people is Replacement Theology. An erroneous teaching which misinformed Christians and resulted in some Christians (or in some cases those who were Christians in name only) mistreating and persecuting Jewish people.

Contrary to what is taught with Replacement Theology, Christians were not sent to replace the Jewish people. During the Dark Ages under orders the Roman priests were directed by the Roman Emperor Constantine to teach the lie God was done with the Jewish people.

Around 325 A.D. the Emperor Constantine of the Imperial Roman Empire or government decided after having a vision he thought was from God, even though he himself was a pagan and worshipped false gods, decided to make it a law everyone would become a Christian. He put this into law and if anyone opposed it they were to be killed. This confirms his vision was not of the True and Living God.

Constantine proceeded to stop all the house church meetings and bring everyone into buildings. All instruction had to come from a few set-in leadership roles placed by Constantine who told them what to tell the people. Tithing was forbidden, celebrating God's Feasts were removed, the presence of the Holy Spirit with the evidence of speaking in other tongues was forbidden, I Cor. 14; Acts 2:4. Reading, teaching and ministering to one another in their home churches were stopped as well.

Constantine also changed the Biblical calendar to the Gregorian calendar (January to December) which the Western cultures use to this day. Since God is the only One that can set the times and seasons God continued with the calendar He set in place. The Jewish people also continued with God's calendar and His Feasts. *They were chosen by God to be a holy nation of people. Holy means set apart and special.*

They witness to the world there is a God in Heaven for the mere fact no empire, however great, has been able to destroy or annihilate them because of God's love and purpose for them. He has protected them and gives them great favor and divine wisdom to produce and achieve in all areas even though they are few in number. Because they are small in comparison to other larger nations they are considered a great nation because of what God has done for them as many of them have chosen to trust and honor Him and His Holy Scriptures.

Since the **pagans became Christians against their will** they refused to give up their worship of their idols. So these false gods were incorporated into what we know today as the *Catholic Church.* Where the names of these idols were changed as they continued to worship their gods in the form of statues with names that began with the title of saint. Consequently, these actions weakened the structure Jesus placed in the earth with the fivefold ministry gifts for His church, Eph. 4:11-12.

Most Christians are not aware the early church started with the twelve apostles selected by the Messiah (Christ) Himself and it was called "The Way." He said, "I am the Way and the Truth and the Life; no one comes to the Father except by (through) Me" John 14:6.   Thousands of Jewish people followed His ministry but most of the Jewish leadership had a problem with the Messiah and the anointing, for He is the Anointed One.

They found religion, traditions, and customs could not stand against the anointing (the power of God). They realized they would lose their influence, authority and power over the people, so they decided to conceal the identity of Jesus the Messiah (Yeshua HaMashiach).

This Man Jesus was God incarnate (God in the form of a human being) who came to the earth. *He was conceived by the power of the Holy Spirit who placed His prepared body with perfect blood for the redemption in a young Jewish girl's womb,* Hebrews 10:5-10. Her name was Miriam or Miryam in Hebrew; Maryam in Greek Luke 1:26-33; and Mary in English.

He was born in Bethlehem at the appointed time for fulfillment of prophecy to redeem mankind and bring them back into relationship with God the Father, Matthew 1:18-23; Romans 5:8-19. **Because this plan was carried out by God Himself it could not fail.** God chose the genealogy for the Messiah (His Son) to come through the Jewish line which included Abraham, Judah, Ruth, King David, Solomon and others and listed it in the New Testament (New Covenant) in the books of Matthew and Luke.

After much persecution and wars, and with a remnant standing for righteousness to protect the Jewish faith given to them by Father God, Jesus/Yeshua was born and became the Light of the World and a Savior for all who chose Him to be their Lord.

Christians were sent to be a branch on the tree (represented by the Jewish people) which is deep rooted and a support as the foundation of Christianity, Romans 11:11-16. In other words, the Christian was grafted into God's family and covenant by the mercy of God, Romans 11:17-19 and then adopted by the Father, Eph. 1:5; Romans 8:15; Psalm 27:10.

Jesus Himself confirmed the New Covenant in I Corinthians 11:25-26 which was spoken of in Jeremiah 31:31-33 that God would make with the house of Israel. And besides all this God promised Israel would return to their land and they did after nearly two thousand years they became a nation on May 14, 1948, Ezekiel 11:14-20.

"No New Testament author suggested in any way that the Hebrew Scriptures were obsolete, and neither did Y'shua. Y'shua/Jesus is quoted in Jn. 10:16 as saying, But I also have sheep which are not from this sheepfold: and it is necessary for Me to lead those and they will hear My voice, and they will become one flock, one shepherd. Y'shua was speaking to the Jewish people referring to the heathens as the other flock. In Matt. 5:18 Y'shua said not one yod or vav would drop from Torah until the sky and the earth would pass away" (The One New Man Bible). Yod and Vav are the two smallest letters in the Hebrew alphabet.

To further make this point, the following is an illustration of a family which has children and chooses to adopt other children. Does the adopted child *replace* the natural children? Of course not, the adopted child is a *welcome addition into the family.* Even if the adopted child came *first,* once a child is born into the family the natural biological addition does not replace the adopted first child in the home. On the contrary, they have the opportunity of becoming one big happy family! Ephesians 2:14-20.

Another illustration is Israel as the olive tree is rooted and Christians are the branches that bear the fruit on the tree. Neither can really function properly without the other. The branches need the root to support it and the tree needs the branches to produce its fruit. In Romans 11:11-25 it illustrates the olive tree and its branches that were broken off. When this happened wild olive branches were grafted in. However, ultimately the original branches will be grafted back in. That was always the plan to make room for other branches and they share the riches of the olive tree.

In addition to the New Covenant we realize it was never God's plan to separate the Jews and Christians. So, in His infinite wisdom *His plan is to reunite the two people groups* that were separated by evil men who served the lessor god.

He will Reunite the Two, Ephesians 2:14-16,

For He is [Himself] our peace (our bond of unity and harmony). He has made us both [Jew and Gentile] one [body], and has broken down (destroyed, abolished) the hostile dividing wall between us, By abolishing in His [own crucified] flesh the enmity [caused by] the Law with its decrees and ordinances [which He annulled]; that **He from the two might create in Himself one new man [one new quality of humanity out of the**

two], so making peace. And [He designed] to reconcile to God both [Jew and Gentile, united] in a single body by means of His cross, thereby killing the mutual enmity *and* bringing the feud to an end. (Emphasis added.)

When this happens they, whether Jew or Gentile, become a Christian Believer in the Messiah, The One New Man, and have begun their walk in Messiah! The message of the One New Man will help us live in covenant revelation.

Last but not least, **Jesus never once denied He was a Jew.** He identified Himself with His own people in John 4:22 NIV. He was born to Jewish parents, however not having the blood of his earthly step-father Joseph but of His Heavenly Father (Hebrew 10:5) as His mother's pregnancy was announced to her by the angel Gabriel Luke 1:26, 30-31. Jesus was circumcised on the eighth day in keeping with Jewish tradition, Luke 2:21. He also had His bar mitzvah on His 13th birthday, Luke 2:41-50; and finally, He kept the Law of Moses and wore the prayer shawl Moses commanded all Jewish men to wear, Matthew 5:17; Mark 6:56 CJB.

He was born a Jew, He died a Jew, He rose from the grave a Jew and He will return as the Lion of the Tribe of Judah, Revelation 5:5. Judah and Jew are derived from the same root word. Remember, our spiritual inheritance owes its very existence to Judaism and a young Jewish Rabbi named Yeshua (Jesus) born in Bethlehem and raised in Nazareth. Paul said in Romans 15:25-27, "…For if the Gentiles have shared in the Jew's spiritual blessings, they owe it to the Jews to share with them their material blessings."

Knowing these few facts, should make it impossible for anyone to say I am a Christian and yet not love or appreciate the Jewish people. Christians who choose to bless the Jews and Israel and pray for Jerusalem will be blessed according to the Word of God which includes not only material blessings but the Lord's favor and protection as well, Psalm 122:6. In Genesis 12:3 **God said to Abram, "I will bless those who bless you, and whoever curses you I will curse…"** Personally, I prefer to be on the receiving end that allows God's plan to work and to be a blessing in my life.

Jewish people are forerunners that went through the *storm,* so Christians would know what to do by the Jewish people's examples of faith, success and failures. If they were perfect there would not have been anything to write about. Furthermore, I don't know of any perfect Christians. However, I do know all people groups need a

Savior, Jew and non-Jews (Gentiles or the nations) alike.

Religion, tradition and customs have taught hundreds of thousands how to operate in their family and in the church. But the church, which functions as the Kingdom of God, belongs to Christ the Anointed One.

The church moves by the leading of Holy Spirit Who is sent by Father God with instructions from He and Jesus. The Spirit of Truth (Holy Spirit) then operates with us in whatever capacity we need Him to be, a Counselor, Helper, Advocate, Intercessor, Strengthener and Standby to lead, guide, teach, reveal, vindicate, convict and much more, John 16:7-14.

Believers do not belong to a religion, traditions or customs of men and if they do then they are operating with a religious spirit. God does not function within religion or traditions. He is Anointed and is outside of the "box."

Therefore, let Him through the power of Holy Spirit teach you how to function both within the family and the Kingdom of God. This is one of the paramount reasons why we should have a close and personal relationship with Father God through Christ Jesus. Being sensitive to His presence and knowing His will, will make all the difference in our walk and fellowship with the True and Living God.

Chapter 7

The King of kings and You

Jesus is an Intimate Personal God

Jesus comes to us as Lord and Savior but also as Family and a Friend. He is not controlling and over powering with people in any way. He lets people come to Him freely because there is liberty in Christ. When He was incarnate He was obedient all the way to the cross as He laid His life down for all of us.

Jesus as a True Friend, John 15:15-16 says,

No longer do I call you servants, for a servant does not know what his master is doing; but I have called you friends, for all things that I heard from My Father I have made known to you. You did not choose Me, but I chose you and appointed you that you should go and bear fruit, and *that* your fruit should remain, that whatever you ask the Father in My name He may give you.

Furthermore, He was supportive and He loved to have the children come to Him. Everyone was important men, women and children. He loved justice, righteousness, integrity and He was always yielded to the Father Himself and His will for His life.

He is the King of kings, yet He was humble enough to become a servant. He even washed the feet of His disciples. Our Lord is the King of heaven and yet in His own words, He said, "For even the Son of Man did not come to be served, but to serve..." Mark 10:45 NKJV.

Once we are aware of His love and sacrifice for us and we wish to serve and thank Him, how would we accomplish this? An example would be Bartimaeus, a blind beggar who instantly received his sight through the power of God, Mark 10:46-52; Luke 18:35-43. "The moment he had been loved, served, and blessed by the Lord, he willingly and without hesitation followed the Savior! And that's how our service to the Lord ought to be out of the overflow of receiving His love for us.

Jesus Himself said, 'Freely you have received, freely give' (Matt. 10:8). We can only give freely of ourselves to God, to His work, and to people He loves (not grudgingly or out of obligation or a misplaced fear of His judgment) when we first freely received His love."

Yeshua is the God of creation yet and still He knows each one of us intimately by name and even knows the number of hairs on our heads. We were wonderfully made! The Word of God tells us, "For

You formed my inward parts; You covered me in my mother's womb. I will praise You, for I am fearfully *and* wonderfully made; Marvelous are Your works, And *that* my soul knows very well," Psalm 139:13-14, NKJV.

Furthermore, God has a free will and He gave us a free will because we were created in His image. We are special and unique and were set apart, so we could have a deep and intimate personal relationship with God the Father through His Son Jesus/Yeshua. He would like us to live with, through and for Him. We were also created for His pleasure and delight as well as His service and glory. For millions and billions know Him as Abba Father, Healer, Friend, their First Love, and/or simply know Him as Someone that is Family!

To know Him in an intimate personal way will happen from the relationship you and He are building together. A couple of ways to start building that relationship would be to seek Him in His Word to learn His will and follow His instructions. And knowing we were also created to fellowship with Him, as we spend time in His presence we can experience His glory. "He gives us life as a gift, and if we will freely offer it back to Him, then and only then can we live it fully and joyfully."

What you experience cannot just be in your mind, you would have to experience Him for yourself in your heart and spirit, knowing that you know, that you know, He is close. By being conscious of His presence; by being aware of His unconditional love for you; by experiencing His power moving on your behalf in time all these things will bring you into the knowledge that you do know Him.

Also, discovering your identity in Him will take you on a journey of first discovering Who He is. Knowing Him intimately is also knowing His character. That He is faithful, loving, forgiving, holy, and so much more! That He only speaks truth and life and He will be with you through every test or trial and is able to give you the victory over it. A part of knowing Who He is, is also knowing how powerful He is, Job 38.

The Word Describes Another Way We Can Know We Know Him, I John 2:4-6,

> Whoever says, I know Him [I perceive, recognize, understand, and am acquainted with Him] but fails to keep *and* obey His commandments (teachings) is a liar, and the Truth [of the Gospel] is not in him. But he who keeps (treasures) His Word [who bears in mind His precepts, who observes His message in its entirety], truly in him has the love of *and* for God been perfected (completed, reached maturity). By this we may

perceive (know, recognize, and be sure) that we are in Him:

Whoever says he abides in Him ought [as a personal debt] to walk *and* conduct himself in the same way in which He walked *and* conducted Himself.

Furthermore, remember there is "no condemnation (no adjudging guilty of wrong) for those who are in Christ Jesus, *who live [and] walk not after the dictates of the flesh, but after the dictates of the Spirit.* For the Law of the Spirit of life [which is] in Christ Jesus [the law of our new being] has freed me from the law of sin and death," Romans 8:1-2.

We do not have to carry guilt or be ashamed of our past before Him, for He knows all things from the beginning to the end of what each one do. He chose to go to the cross and die for our sins anyway. And He kept us from that horrible end of where sin would take us, Romans 6:23; James 1:15; I John 5:17.

"He dealt perfectly with the payment and punishment of all the wrong that you and I have done and will ever do." Now He asks us to pardon one another as He has freely forgiven us.

It Says in Colossians 3:13-15,

Be gently *and* forbearing with one another and, if one has a difference (a grievance or complaint) against another, readily pardoning each other; even as the Lord has [freely] forgiven you, so must you also [forgive].

And above all these [put on] love *and* enfold yourselves with the bond of perfectness [which binds everything together completely in ideal harmony].

And let the peace (soul harmony which comes from Christ rule (act as umpire continually) in your hearts ... And be thankful (appreciative), [giving praise to God always].

Building and Embracing a Personal Relationship with Messiah

In order to embrace a personal relationship with our Heavenly Father which was made possible through His Beloved Son, Christ Jesus we are given certain instructions. These instructions will lead and show us how to come into God's presence as we grow closer to Him to achieve a relationship with our Creator.

The King Left So We Could Come Closer in Fellowship with the Comforter, John 16:7,

> However, I am telling you nothing but the truth when I say it is profitable (good, expedient, advantageous) for you that I go away. Because if I do not go away, the Comforter (Counselor, Helper, Advocate, Intercessor, Strengthener, Standby) will not come to you [into close fellowship with you]; but if I go away, I will send Him to you [*to be in close fellowship with you*]. (Emphasis added.)

To build and maintain a close relationship with Father God will require knowing, receiving and close fellowship through the Divine Third Person of the Trinity, Holy Spirit, Who is the Spirit of Truth!

John 16:13-15 says,

> But when He, the Spirit of Truth (the Truth-giving Spirit) comes, He will guide you into all Truth (the whole, full Truth). For He will not speak His own message [on His own authority]; but He will tell whatever He hears [from the

Father; He will give the message that has been given to Him], and He will announce *and* declare to you the things that are to come [that will happen in the future]. He will honor *and* glorify Me, because He will take of (receive, draw upon) what is Mine and will reveal (declare, disclose, transmit) it to you. Everything that the Father has is Mine. That is what I meant when I said that He [the Spirit] will take the things that are Mine and will reveal (declare, disclose, transmit) it to you.

We are to have a close and personal relationship with Holy Spirit which will bring us closer to our Heavenly Father and to His Son, Christ Jesus. This is accomplished as we fellowship with Holy Spirit Who speaks to us on their behalf.

Holy Spirit is in charge of the affairs of the Kingdom of God on the earth. He is responsible for bringing mankind into the knowledge and things of God giving them true, vision, guidance, protection and shalom (wholeness). True peace comes because one is whole. As you encounter Holy Spirit it will literally transform your life.

Therefore, those with a life of routine, greed, lust, hopelessness and fear are brought to a life that is full and one that includes love, joy, peace, patience and more as they develop a relationship with Holy Spirit who will lead you to worship, praise and glorify the King of kings. (See *God's Way and Spiritual Warfare* for more exciting news about Holy Spirit.)

With a personal relationship with Jesus, God's purpose for your life, vision, dream or assignment will come alive with clarity, instructions, provision, power and the grace, the enablement to fulfill it, because of your intimate relationship with Him.

The Bible says without revelation knowledge My people perish, they are destroyed, they can become confused, their mind wanders, they become wild and have a lack of purpose and live with a life full of regrets, Hosea 4:6. By staying close to Jesus keeping their eyes on Him their vision will stay alive and come forth at the appointed time Habakkuk 2:2-3.

As you and your family flow and operate in God's order each day, a complete work will be accomplished in your life. To have true success and victory make a choice to follow Jesus, stay focused and live holy (upright) with the help of Holy Spirit because you are set apart for God's purpose.

Remember Jesus will not force anyone to choose His way. You must not only be willing to allow God's standard and order to operate in your life but be willing to have certain things or people pruned from your life and lifestyle as well. For those who decide to follow, He will empower them to be blessed and become a blessing to others.

He will also place divine connections across your path to enable you to prosper and many of these connections will be in positions of authority, in different businesses, civil agencies, at your work place and so on. Many times, these people will be complete strangers and as you respect the delegated authority before you God will open doors of opportunity.

This would entail putting off the "old man" (the old person) and learning how to renew your mind in Christ, Romans 12:2. This brings about dying to fleshly desires that are sent to tempt you into bondage and sin and eventually lead you off or from the path God has for your life. This does not mean that certain relationships that were removed will be permanent for some will be reinstated at the appointed time and it will be better than it previously was.

The Goodness of God

There is no such thing as luck in the Kingdom of God. We are blessed on purpose because of the goodness of God! Some are just not sure how Good He is. They have their opinions of Who He is and what He will do and if He will do anything for them. Truly spoken by someone who does not know Him.

God said He is the same yesterday, today and forever, Heb. 13:8. If you follow His ways, and have patience seeking what it is He is desiring to impart in you and hold your course you will experience a breakthrough and taste and see just how *good* the Lord really is.

Stop blaming God for every mistake or every hard thing or every bad thing that happens. Remember you have an adversary and your flesh (your mind) dictating to you which way you should go. Don't allow your bitterness to turn you against God and believe Him to be anything other than Who He truly is. Choose to even forgive God if you think He is your problem.

When we simply if we yield to the right way to go, which is kingdom thinking (Mt. 6:33) a way will be made on that path because God is righteous and He knows the right way to go. He is a just God.

He also uses favor to open doors when the time is right and all the right connections are in place. His favor stems from His goodness. His favor will produce supernatural increase, promotions, restoration, give honor, real estate and so forth. He knows how to give and how to cause you to keep what He has given. That is why preparation and study are vital in order to receive and maintain.

His goodness protects us. Just think of what could have happened to your life if it were not for His goodness. Especially if you are peaceful, calm, strong, confident, victorious and happy even during confusion and difficult circumstances.

I Once Heard Someone Describe the Goodness God According to their Perception and I would like to Reiterate a Portion of It:

"He is the First and the Last, the Beginning and the End. He is the Keeper of creation and creator of all. He is the architect of the universe and the manager of all time. He always was, always is and always will be unmoved, unchanged, undefeated, and never undone. He was bruised but brought healing, He was pierced but eased pain, He was persecuted to death but brings life, He was risen to bring power and raised to bring peace. The world can't understand Him, armies can't defeat Him, schools can't explain Him and leaders can't ignore Him. He is life, He is love, He is longevity, He is the Lord. He is Goodness and Kindness, and Faithfulness and He is God. He is Holy and righteous and powerful and pure. His ways are right, His Word is eternal, His will unchanging and His mind is on us. His yoke is easy, His burden is light and His goal for us is abundant life. I follow Him because He is the wisdom of the wise, power of the powerful, the ancient of Days, the Ruler of rulers and the leader of all leaders. His goal is a relationship with me. He will never leave you, forsake you, never mislead you, never forget or overlook you and never cancel your appointment in His appointment book. When you fall He will lift you up, when you fail He will forgive you. When you are week He is strong, when you are lost He is your way. When you are hurt He will heal you, when you are broken He will mend you and when you face trials He is with you. When we face loss, He will provide for us and when we all face death He will carry us all home to meet Him. He is everything for everybody, everywhere, every time and in every way. He is your God and that is who you belong to!"

Who I Am to Messiah

Most individuals believe things and money can bring them true joy, such as houses and all new furnishings, land, businesses, travel, educational opportunities and degrees, recreation with good food, vehicles, expensive clothes and accessories, the perfect work, the perfect relationship, the perfect family, great vacations or events (weddings, birthday celebrations, grand openings, concerts, museums) and so forth.

Things make a good attempt because happiness will usually follow. However, soon it wears off and the void is still there. But some of us have realized things not even money will fill the void that is in your heart (your spirit). That spot is reserved by the Lord, for the Lord and only He can fill it.

Once you discover something vital is missing in your life, and you simply cannot fill the void in your own strength and you discover it is a personal relationship with your Creator, you can do something to remedy that.

In your search you will discover you are wonderfully made and unique in every way. If you make a choice to join Him and His family a settling peace will come to confirm your decision. Why does this happen? The Holy Spirit has touched your heart. The process to wholeness will begin. Wholeness is described as nothing is missing and nothing is broken in your life, Shalom. I did not say perfect. But you can have a calm and a peace amid of the storms of life because of Who is in you and with you.

Also, in your search for truth, you will find God has a good plan and purpose for your life, Jer. 29:11. You will feel secure knowing He truly has an unconditional love for you. You will know He will never leave you or fail you. That you can trust Him and never have to be alone again in life.

Furthermore, there will not be any need to compare your life to anyone else or to compete with anyone. You can learn to rest in what He is doing with your life, knowing you have favor and the grace that will enable you to continue and become successful. His mercy and loving-kindness will be with you every day. To what Jesus has to offer there is no comparison in this earth and the void will be filled at last!

As we seek Him first before seeking His hand for blessings and gifts we will be thankful for having a relationship with Almighty God.

Speak the following declarations out loud into the atmosphere and let it go into your ears and down into your heart (spirit) and soul and experience the assurance of *knowing who you are to Messiah and some of the things He has done for you.*

I Am:

1. A child of God and I am not of this world, Romans 8:16; John 17:16
2. A new creature, the old previous moral & spiritual condition has passed away, 2 Cor 5:17
3. Blessed with all spiritual blessings in heavenly places in Christ, Eph. 1:3

4. Justified, Sanctified and created in His image, Ro. 5:1; I Cor 6:11; Ro. 8:29

5. In covenant with God and He is merciful not to remember my sins any more, Heb. 8:10,12

6. Asking God for His forgiveness daily, receiving it and forgiving others, I John 1:9

7. Heir to the Blessing [promised] to Abraham, Gal. 3:14

8. Blessed coming in and blessed going out, Deut. 28:6

9. An heir of God and a joint heir with Jesus, Romans 8:17

10. A son of God and I am led by the Holy Spirit, Ro. 8: 13-14

11. Not condemned because I am in Christ Jesus, Ro. 8:1

12. Redeemed and forgiven through His blood, Col. 1:14

13. Redeemed from the hand of the enemy, Psalm, 107:2

14. Daily overcoming the devil, I John 4:4

15. Submitted to God, therefore, when I resist the devil he must flee, James 4:7

16. Exercising my authority over the enemy, Luke 10:19

17. An overcomer by the Blood of the Lamb and the Word of my Testimony, Rev. 12:10-11

18. Redeemed from the curse of the Law, Gal. 3:13

19. Delivered from the powers of darkness, Col. 1:13

20. Destroying the works of the devil, I John 3:8

21. Free from all fear because perfect love casts out fear, I John 4:18
22. Doing all things through Christ who strengthens me, Phil. 4:13
23. Casting down vain imaginations and bringing into captivity every thought to obedience to Christ Jesus, 2 Cor. 10:5
24. Using the mind of Christ; Studying to show myself approved of God, I Co. 2:16; 2 Tim. 2:15
25. Being transformed by a renewing of my mind, Ro. 12:1, 2
26. Keeping my mind set on what is above (the higher things) not things on this earth, Col. 3:2
27. Partaker of His Divine Nature; called with a Holy calling, 2 Peter 1:4; 2 Tim. 1:9
28. Called, Chosen and Faithful, Rev. 17:14
29. Strong in the Lord and in the Power of His Might, Eph. 6:10
30. Wearing the Whole Armor of God and praying in the Holy Spirit daily, Eph. 6:12-18
31. Walking by faith and not by sight; I am the light of the world, 2 Cor. 5:7; Mt. 5:14
32. Saved by grace through faith because I am of God's household of faith, Eph. 2:8; Gal. 6:10
33. Walking in Love and living by faith, I Cor. 13 and Ro. 1:17
34. Strong in faith, giving glory to God, not wavering with doubt or unbelief, Romans 4:20
35. Fighting the good fight of faith, I Tim. 6:12
36. Not moved by what I see, Ro. 4:19
37. Above only and not beneath, Deut. 28:13

38. More than a conqueror; nothing can separate me from the love of God, Ro. 8:37; Ro. 8:35
39. In this hour receiving double portion, Isa. 61:7
40. Witnessing my sons and daughters receive blessings and deliverance, Joel 2:28, 32
41. In a God-fearing Family that is walking in their new assignment, Ps. 128:1-4; Isa. 43:19
42. Expecting my children to keep their lives pure and in accordance with the Lord, Ps. 119:11
43. Expecting my nation to remain a Christian nation and keep biblical practices, 2 Chr. 7:14
44. Declaring no weapon formed against my household or country will prosper, Isa. 54:17
45. Casting all my cares on Jesus and remaining well balanced, I Peter 5:7-8
46. Living the joyful and abundant life Jesus came to give me, John 10:10
47. Blessed because I am observing and doing the Lord's will for my life, Deut. 28:12
48. Empowered to get wealth, Deut. 8:18
49. An inheritor of eternal life, I John 5:11, 12
50. Filled with the Holy Spirit with the evidence of my Heavenly language, Acts 2:4, 39
51. Complete in Him, Col. 2:10
52. Filled with the knowledge of His will in all wisdom and spiritual understanding, Col. 1:9
53. A doer of the Word   Jas. 1:22
54. Increasing in the knowledge of God, Col. 1:10
55. Letting His Truth set me free, John 8:32, 36
56. Blessed because I hear the Word of God and practice it, Luke 11:28
57. Established in Righteousness, Isa. 54:14

58. The righteousness of God and acceptable and in right relationship with Him, 2 Cor. 5:21

59. A laborer together with God, I Cor. 3:9

60. Kept in safety at all times because I live in the Secret Place of the Most High, Ps. 91: 1, 11

61. Healed by His stripes because God wants me to prosper in every way, I Peter 2:24; 3 John 2

62. Establishing God's Word here on earth, Matt. 16:19

63. Loving God with all my heart, soul, strength and mind, Luke 10:27

64. In love with God and I am His friend, I John 4:19; John 14:15 and John 15:14

65. Abiding in His Love and showing His love towards others, I John 4:16 and I Cor. 13:4-8

66. Loved by God, John 3:16

67. Crowned in His loving kindness and tender mercies, Ps. 103

68. Free from the law of sin and death, Romans 8:32

69. Strong in the Grace that is in Christ Jesus, 2 Tim. 2:1

70. Building my house upon the Rock, Mt. 7:24-25

71. Trusting in the Lord acknowledging Him in all my ways, Prov. 3:5-7

72. Honoring the Lord with all my capital and sufficiency from righteous labors and with the firstfruits of all my income, Prov. 3:9; Mal 3:10; Luke 14:13, 14

73. Pressing on to His high calling, Phil. 3:14

74. Receiving all the Promises of God, 2 Cor. 1:20
75. Abiding in His rest as I seek first the Kingdom of God, Heb. 4:3; Mt. 6:33
76. Holding my confidence which has a great & glorious compensation of reward, Heb. 10:35
77. Walking in the Wisdom of God, James 1:5
78. The Elect of God, Col. 3:12
79. In everything giving Thanks to Christ Jesus for this is His will for me, I Thess. 5:18
80. Adopted into the family of God through Jesus Christ, Eph. 1:5

Foundational Points to Mature in Christ Jesus as We Become Sons and Daughters

- **Receive Jesus/Yeshua** as your Lord and Savior (Romans 10:9; Acts 2:21; John 10:9). (See *Appendix A* for a Prayer for Salvation.)

- **Receive the "Infilling of the Holy Spirit"** also known as the "Baptism in the Holy Spirit" with the evidence of speaking in your supernatural prayer language aka tongues. When we pray in the spirit we edify ourselves (improve or uplift). It also strengthens us and builds us up in our faith. We are praying above what we know in our natural minds because the Holy Spirit is praying for and through you. It also opens the door to revelation, wisdom, instructions and encouragement. (Acts 2:1-8; Romans 8:9-11; I Corinthians 14:2; 2:4-5, Jude 20:1). (See *Appendix C* for more information regarding having your supernatural prayer language and its benefits.)

- **Develop a personal relationship** with Him through your prayer life as you commune with Him through His Holy Spirit; read and study His Word; and as you pay attention and follow His teachings you will be blessed (Matthew 7:7; 2 Tim. 2:15; Deut. 28:1-14).

- **Join a local Christian Church**, one that is Spirit-filled and studies the Word through the Holy Bible and considers themselves to be a part of God's Kingdom. Being a part of a local church will give you the proper covering you need as you begin your walk or journey with God. It is important to have people to come in agreement with you who are mature in the things of God and who can feed you the Word with revelation on a regular basis to help you acquire understanding and unfold mysteries. "...Christ brings us together as a family. Christians seek ways to encourage one another to express love through good deeds. Communal worship is one way we gain strength and motivation from other disciples." [1] Hebrews 10:24-25.

- **Hebrews 10:25 KJV Tells Us Not to Give Up Meeting Together,** "Not forsaking the assembling of ourselves together, as the manner of some is; but exhorting one another: and so much the more, as ye see the day approaching."

- As you are **learning of Him and renewing your mind** in the Word of God seek Him for His purpose and will for your life. Stay open and receive confirmation and once you start to receive information about your assignment (purpose or vision) write it down so it can be clear, so Satan cannot come and steal it from your memory over a period of time, Habakkuk 2:2-3. Now ask God for His instructions, directions, will, strength and desire while you are on your journey to ensure reaching your destiny.

- **Attend a good Bible study class regularly.** Also attend conferences and conventions as you are led by Holy Spirit. Coming together in conferences is very powerful.

- **Watch Christian programs,** there are many available. If you do not know of any may I suggest *Trinity Broadcasting Network,* www.TBN.org. It is the largest Christian television network in the world. They own a family of twenty-four Christian networks.

Their networks reach out to the lost, families, children, teens, churches and other countries in their own languages around the world. They offer a variety of programs, live streams, on demand Christian videos and movies, ministry teachings and a lot more 24/7 in most places.

- **Read Christian books; listen to CD's** and watch DVD's on the latest technology. Develop relationships with people God has placed across your path to become mentors, prayer partners, friends and to possibly form a Spiritual Family. Reading and using materials that are non-Christian are fine; everything is from above but realize some materials have become twisted, perverted and are demonic so guard what you allow into your soul through your eyes and ears. Some self-help books and materials are alright, many of them are biblically based but without scripture references and mixed with a lot of *opinions of men* offering information that is not a biblical standard to live by.

- Allow Holy Spirit to **train you up to resist evil in this spiritual war** so you will walk in the victory that has already been given to you over the kingdom of darkness, Ps 119:115; I John 4:4. Because of your covenant with God when you use your authority acquired because of the finished work at the cross realize He has already "disarmed the principalities and powers that were ranged against you and made a bold display and public example of them…" Col.2:15 paraphrased. (See *God's Way and Spiritual Warfare.*)

- Declare daily you are **covered with the Blood of Jesus** (Revelation 12:11; Exodus 12:13) and you have on the *Whole Armor of God* which does include your supernatural prayer language aka speaking in tongues as shown in Ephesians 6:10-18.

- Be mindful that walking (living) with **the fruit of the Spirit** will enable you to express in your daily life the character of God, Gal. 5:22-23. Others will see the glory of God on you even if they do not know what it is they are seeing. They will conclude there is something different about you.

- **Are You Seeking His Hand or His Face?** It is important to seek God for Who He is. Welcome His Presence. Worship Him in praise and by being obedient to His will (His plans, instructions and teachings). Desire to know Him. It is perfectly fine to ask about your needs and desires. And inquire about other things, pray for leaders, others and so forth. But **we must remember to be**

thankful. Being sincere with a grateful heart will unlock the blessings of God. Being thankful will increase your faith. Acknowledging God will give you favor and will open doors for your future. Being thankful will bring you into the Presence of God. It can also prepare the way for you to have a deeper relationship with the Lord.

- **The Bottom Line** –There are several Habits strong Christian Believers should form and maintain such as: **Read** God's Word to feed your spirit man, Mt. 4:4 and John 16:33. Start with a small number of pages and increase. The point is to get started, so do what you can. Many never start because they cannot see how they can finish quickly or achieve their goal, Zech. 4:10. **Build** your faith up, Romans 10:17; Heb. 11:33-34; I Sam. 30:6; Romans 10:17; Ro. 1:7; 2 Cor. 5:7; Jude 1:20. **Speak** the Word of God. Speak healing, blessing, peace, forgiveness, abundance, life and not death, truth, nobility, justice and purity. You will have what you speak, Mark 11:23, Matthew 7:7; Phil. 4:8. For life and death are in the power of the tongue, Prov. 18:21. Control your **thought life** (Joshua, 1:8). Dr. Caroline Leaf (http://drleaf.com/) shared about the connection between thoughts and overall success in life. To take control of your thoughts she says, "Thoughts are real things – they occupy real estate in your brain. 'Bring all thoughts into captivity.' Our brain is designed to do that. And when you do… your brain [will] start operating correctly," 2 Cor. 10:4-5; Romans 12:2. As we study the Word of God it will heal your physical brain. The Word of God is living words that are anointed with the power of God to bring life, healing and wholeness. **Praise the Lord,** as we were created to do so. Praising the Lord is a form of prayer and a language of faith and receiving, Psalm 34:1; Ps. 100:4. **Praying in the Spirit** we edify and strengthen ourselves, as mentioned above (Also see *Appendix C* for more information.) **Putting former things behind us** and letting go of the past and receiving healing for our emotions, as we mature in the things of God and move forward, Isa. 43:18-19; Heb. 12:1; Romans 12:2; Phil. 4:8.

As you do your part, be confident He will fulfill His. He has made certain promises He cannot break because He is a God that cannot lie. Therefore, if you do not break the covenant by living outside of His will with an unrepentant heart be prepared for the promise to come to pass at the appointed time.

Claim your protection and comfort as you learn and grow neigh to your heavenly Father. Confess and receive Bible verses such as Psalm 91:1 which says, *"He who dwells in the secret place of the Most High shall remain stable and fixed under the shadow of the Almighty [whose power no foe can withstand]."* And in Psalm 91:7 "A thousand may fall at my side and ten thousand at my right hand, but it shall not come near you." For Comfort, also see Psalms 23; Ps. 46:10; Isa. 41:10 and 2 Chron. 20:15-17.

Rewards and Benefits Come to Responsible People

Responsibility requires discipline. With godly discipline we can successfully steward over what God has entrusted to us. The responsibility begins with our own bodies (temple) where He dwells within us when we are Born-again Christian Believers.

As we are responsible to govern ourselves by keeping God first in our life the Lord will impart the wisdom to keep balance in everything else that is our responsibility. The more we lean on His wisdom and understanding the more He can trust true riches with us. The good life, the higher life in Christ!

Strive to take care of your body working with the Holy Spirit as He guides you in proper diet, rest, exercise, dress and how you carry yourself. He may give you an unction of what to do or a check in your spirit as to what may be harmful or unacceptable for you. He will place information across your path if you seek His help. Giving you what to read, watch with the correct information and what to eat and not to eat, as well as when to rest and have recreation in your life in addition to work.

In today's societies stress and pressure dominate but in the Kingdom of God as we trust God we will find we do not have to work under such conditions and risk our health and possibly destroy the temple in which we carry the Light of the world. We need to let our light shine not have it put out because of bad habits and lack of discipline. Remember, we represent the Kingdom of God and our King, Lord and Savior Christ Jesus.

Be mindful to seek and trust Him for direction and the purpose of your life. He gave you life, and sent you and He does not do anything without purpose. As we discover our purpose and walk in it with His help (more than likely it is something you cannot accomplish without Him) the fulfillment so many crave and hunger for will be fulfilled.

Basic discipline formed out of good habits and wisdom will cause one to be responsible and people that are responsible will be given leadership roles in life. They will be given more responsibility as they mature. They will be given power when they are responsible simply because God can trust them with His authority and power.

Responsible people are willing to go the distance to prepare themselves with a prayer life, study of the Word of God, education and/or training wherever it is necessary to achieve the goals placed in their heart.

Accumulating a lot of information is useless if you are not in touch with the One who can give you revelation to know what to do with all the information you are acquiring. It is not for the purpose of being puffed up but to help others achieve their endeavors in life. It is for God's will.

As you are responsible He can download more into your vessel knowing a good outcome will be the result. Taking responsibility also means we own up to our own shortcomings or mistakes. Therefore, try not to complain and blame others.

Renew Your Mind and be Transformed, Romans, 12:2 says,

> Do not be conformed to this world (this age), [fashioned after and adapted to its external, superficial customs], but be transformed (changed) by the [entire] renewal of your mind [by its new ideals and its new attitude], so that you may prove [for yourselves] what is the good and acceptable and perfect will of God, *even* the thing which is good and

acceptable and perfect [in His sight for you].

With clear thinking and right information and revelation, right believing will come and believing right will cause living right. Most of us have already experienced thinking and believing wrongly and it produced wrong living. With God and His ways first, an inward heart transformation will take place and truth with the right fruit will rule.

God is prepared to promote and send out those who are willing to take responsibility for their life and actions. Right living will include perseverance, diligence, exercising faith, exercising virtue, self-control, knowledge, kindness, peace, gentleness, patience, love and joy. In other words, the character of God as found in the fruit of the Spirit, and fruitful growth in the faith, Gal. 5:22-23; 2 Peter 1:5-7.

Freely He gives fruit of the Spirit to every Believer who will strive to develop them in their lives to assume commitment and be the responsible person God called them to be.

Unfortunately, there are Believers who lack these qualities. But with discipline they can be obtained and developed so they can accept their responsibilities in life. The choice is always ours. "We should no longer be children, tossed to and fro and carried about with every wind of doctrine, by the trickery of men, in the cunning craftiness of deceitful plotting," (Eph. 4:14) and not taking on our responsibilities in life.

Speak the Truth in Love, Eph. 4:15 says,

> Rather, let our lives lovingly express truth [in all things, speaking truly, dealing truly, living truly]. Enfolded in love, let us grow up in every way *and* in all things into Him Who is the Head, [even] Christ (the Messiah, the Anointed One).

If we hold to Jesus' teachings, it shows we are really His disciples. Those that are really His followers will hold to His Word. For His Words are truth and they are alive and have the power to transform lives, John 8:31.

Guard Your Words as well as Discern Words from the Lord

Remember complaining and murmuring removes your divine protection and favor and it has the power to set you back in your endeavors (Phil 2:14; I Co 10:10; Prov.18:20-21). It will push you further away from His presence rather than bring you closer to Him. It is a sin before God and one should repent.

Since words are "spirit" the spirit realm takes every word as a command or a mandate that we speak. How the word is spoken or expressed does not make a difference. For example, if it is said seriously, as a joke, as a decree or demand it does not matter because the words have been released into the atmosphere (the spiritual realm) and they will eventually bring you a harvest of whatever you are saying.

We have what we say because we are normally saying what is in our heart. Words do not return to God void. When you speak His words, they become fruitful. When you speak negative, evil and so forth types of words they produce a harvest too, just not the type of harvest that is pleasing for people.

Therefore, guard what you say because the harvest of your words will manifest whether they were godly words or negative ones. By your words you establish life or death, success or failure, peace or chaos, blessings or curses. In addition, when others speak negative, evil words over you and your destiny, do not believe them, do not come in agreement with them because that is not what God has spoken about you or your destiny.

Simply forgive them then reverse their negative words when you pray and cast the negative words down. Rebuke and bind those words up and place them under the blood of Jesus. Replace them with truth and positive words that have been spoken or that are from the Word of God. These steps will aid in cutting off a bad harvest and replacing with a good one because of our changing the words that were spoken into the atmosphere. ***God's Word is the standard we measure all other words by.***

While seeking God and you are not sure which way to go or what to do, be still and continue to wait for clear instructions, guidance and peace. Continue doing what He has already shown you to do. *When some type of action takes place or you receive instructions and you want to make sure it is of God, so that you are on the right track, ask God to confirm it is of Him.* As you continue, you will walk into all and more than you hoped for, at the appointed time.

God speaks when, where and how He chooses to speak. If He chooses to speak through a vessel He has raised up by His Spirit remember people are not perfect and they only have a part of the whole picture and that gifts of the Spirit and the anointing vary from person to person.

So, if you receive a prophetic word and it witnesses to you then receive the Word and act on it at the proper time. If it does not witness in your spirit (heart) then ask God to confirm this word and remain still until further instructions or confirmation arrives. However, if it is a word of encouragement receive it and continue on the path God has placed you on.

All authority in heaven and on earth was given to Jesus and His Words are Spirit and Life, Mt. 28:18; John 6:63. He has given us as Believers all authority in His name and the power to do the works He called each of us to do, Luke 10:19; Job 28:27-28; Prov. 1:1-7. Therefore, we can exercise that authority with the words we speak or confess.

As we guard our words we are choosing to set our day with godly positive words that will release *Life, Faith and Angels.* The words you speak also identify you, they set boundaries in your life and they affect your spirit (your inward man). As you declare, decree or confess (speak) words into the atmosphere they do not return void but will bring a harvest. We have what we believe when we say it, Mark 11:23. Therefore, we should use our authority given to us by Christ and speak words that will produce life and fruit into our situations and for others.

Personalized Word Declaration Examples

I declare You will guard me and keep me in perfect and constant peace because my mind is stayed on You, Isa. 26:3.

I decree wisdom builds my house. I declare I will use wisdom to build my house in Him. I further declare God will reveal mysteries to me as I seek

His wisdom. Let the wisdom of God come in, in Jesus' name, Proverbs chapters 1 -3; I Cor. 14:2.

I declare I am gifted with discernment to avoid deception and bring clear hearing from God to have the ability to discern and distinguish between true spirits and false ones, I Cor. 12:10. As I am granted "a spirit of wisdom and revelation [of insight into mysteries and secrets] in the [deep and intimate] knowledge of Him...", so that I "can know *and* understand the hope to which He has called" me ...And [so that I "can know and understand] what is the immeasurable *and* unlimited *and* surprising greatness of His power in *and* for" me and all who "believe, as demonstrated in the working of His mighty strength" Eph. 1:17-19. As I advance, I am divinely empowered and increase in "skill in all learning and wisdom" and "understanding in all [kinds of] visions and dreams," Dan 1:17.

I decree I will break into what I could not break into in other seasons. I refuse to stay in this wilderness one day past God's appointed time, Hab. 2:3.

I decree these things regarding God's provision in my life: All of my needs are met according to God's riches in Christ Jesus, Phil. 4:19. Lord show me the way I should go and deliver me from my enemies (poverty, lack, hinderances, sickness, and so forth)

Ps. 143:8-12. God blesses me and makes me a blessing to others, Gen. 12:2.

I decree tithers rights over my life. I come in agreement with my love ones and call in the harvest, Mal. 3:10.

As Our Head He is Concerned About Us

Always know and be aware of how much we are loved. *He is concerned about His family and He is concerned about His Kingdom as He oversees them both.* He is the One that is merging the two together especially in this last hour as one strong and magnificent body of people that will rise up and be a voice, the church without spot or wrinkle, Eph. 2:14-16.

He will restore us to a position of power that will take back what the enemy has stolen by giving us great favor, with spiritual weapons, strategies and gifts to use for His will and purposes in doing good.

As our Savior He is our High Priest, Good Shepherd, Groom and Eldest Brother. He is the Head of His family as we are His body, His children, known as His flock of sheep, His bride and joint-heirs with Christ.

As King He is our Lord, Master, Commander-in-Chief, Chief Apostle, and Bishop that will rule His Kingdom with justice and might. He leads and instructs His church to govern, legislate and manage His Kingdom on the earth, Eph. 1:22.

He is our King and we are a remnant, those true worshippers that live for and in Christ Jesus in His Kingdom. We function as sons of God, His partners, citizens of the Kingdom, soldiers in His army and a government. We function as those that walk in His authority, might and power.

Some Things Jesus Endured and Why *Jesus would Understand* what People Endure or Tolerate Due to Persecution because of their Faith: [2]

From an early age, as a carpenter, He knew all about working hard with His hands, standing on His feet all day long and returning home with aches in His body.

He continues to say that, the religious leaders of His day made life difficult for Him. **They challenged His authority (Matt. 21:23) and tested His teachings** (Matt. 19:3). They also called Him a glutton, winebibber, friend of tax collectors and sinners (Matt. 11:19, and blasphemer (Mark 2:7). They said that He was demon-possessed and mad (John 10:20), put Him on the spot when they brought an adulterous woman to Him (John 8:2-11), attempted to stone Him (John 8:59, 10:31-39) and accused Him of perverting the nation (Luke 23:2). He was also chased out of His own hometown (Luke 4:29).

He experienced the pain of being denied by a loved one (Luke 22:54-62) and **betrayed by one considered close to Him** (Luke 22: 47-48). He also knows all about the sickness you are suffering because He bore your sickness and pains on the cross (Isaiah 53:4). He endured His sufferings for our sakes, so that we can have His peace and the anointing to rise above the troubles we are facing.

My friend, you may feel that no one understands your struggles. Listen, while this may be true of man, it is not true of Jesus. He knows exactly what you are going through and He can sympathize with your weaknesses because He was in all points tempted as we are, yet without sin.

None of us have been tempted in all points. But God allowed Jesus to be tempted in all points so that He can understand and identify with the struggles of every single person on this earth. He can be touched by our humanity –our weaknesses, tears, disappointments, griefs…

All Points!

There is no trial, difficulty, challenge or temptation that you face that Jesus cannot identify with. My friend, the moment you go through it, right there and then, He feels it too. That is the kind of representative you have in Jesus! That is the love of God so that you will draw near to His throne of grace (not judgment) to find mercy and grace in time of need! (Hebrews 4:15-16).[3]

What was Finished and Accomplished at the Cross?

The Finished Work at the Cross is where His endurance of persecution and suffering produced a great work beyond measure and no other person has ever done as much for people as our Savior. He stayed focused on His assignment knowing it was a work that would last for eternity and because of His suffering and the price that was paid He knew of the joy that would come out of it and bring Light into the world. He declared **"…It is finished!** And He bowed His head and gave up His Spirit" (John 19:30). Furthermore, the proof of His death was a pierced side where blood and water flowed indicating His heart had ruptured before He died (John 19:34).

Hebrews 12:2 says,

> Looking away [from all that will distract] to Jesus, Who is the Leader *and* the Source of our faith [giving the first incentive for our belief] and is also its Finisher [bringing it to maturity and perfection]. He, for the joy [of obtaining the prize] that was set before Him, endured the cross, despising *and* ignoring the shame, and is now seated at the right hand of the throne of God.

What was Accomplished that Day at Calvary because of His Love, Humility & Determination?

He conquered Death and **He gave us Eternal Life** John 3:16; Rev. 1:18

He took our Sins and **He gave us His Righteousness** 2 Cor. 5:21; Ro. 5:17; John 1:29

He took our Sickness and **He gave us Health** I Peter 2:24; 3 John 2; Isaiah 53:4-5

He took our Brokenness and **He gave us Wholeness,**
 Mark 10:52

He took Confusion and Torment and **He gave us Peace of Mind**
John 14:27; Romans 8:1

He took our Poverty and **He gave us Wealth**
Deut. 8:18; Gal. 3:14; 2 Cor. 8:9

He took the Punishment and **He gave us Forgiveness**
Ephesians 1:17

He took our Weaknesses and **He gave us Strength**
Isaiah 40:31; Romans 8:26

He took the Curses and **He gave us Blessings**
Deut. 28:1-14 and 15-68; Gal. 3:13-14

He took our Lack and **He gave us Prosperity**
Job 36:11; Prov.10:22; Dt.8:18; Jn 10:10; 2 Co. 8:9

He Punished the Wicked and **He gave us Deliverance**
 Prov. 11:21

He Scattered our Enemies and **He gave us Victory**
Luke 23:12; Deut. 28:7

He gave us **Power in the Holy Spirit and Unknown Tongues of fire (power)**
Acts 2:1-4 and 19:6; I Cor. 14:2

He made us **sons of God** as He became the **Son of Man**
Romans 8:14-16

He gave us **Beauty for Ashes**, He gave us the **Oil of Joy** instead of mourning, and He gave us the **Garment of Praise** instead of the spirit of heaviness
Isaiah 61:3

He gave us **Wisdom and Revelation** while others were Spiritually Blind
2 Cor. 4:4; I Co. 2:7-8

He will wipe away every tear and Remove Death, Sorrow and Pain forever **He makes All Things New**
Revelation 21:4-5

He made us the **Head and Not the Tail**
Deut. 28:13

He Who **Comforts** (consoles and encourages) in every trouble (calamity and affliction)
2 Corinthians 1:3-4

He gave us **Authority in His Name** for His Authority is in heaven and on earth
Luke 10:19; Matthew 28:18; Mark 16:17

He caused us to be **Heirs of God**
Romans 8:17

He caused us to be **Overcomers**
Rev. 12:10-11

He is **Close to the Brokenhearted** and saves those who are crushed with sorrow
Psalm 34:18

He **Heals the Brokenhearted** and binds up their wounds [curing their pain and their sorrow]
Psalm 147:3

He **caused us to be the Lender** and not the Borrower
Prov. 22:7

He said **Fear Not I AM with you** I will strengthen you… help you… retain you…with My right hand of righteousness
Isaiah 41:10

He gave us **Reconciliation to God** as
He was Separated from Father God
Ro. 10:9; Acts 2:21; Matt. 27:46; Isaiah 53

He gave us **All the Promises in His Word**
2 Cor. 1:20

"The works of the Lord are great, sought out by all those who have delight in them. His work is honorable and glorious, and His righteousness endures forever," Ps. 111:2-3. The Lord declared in the New Covenant He will be merciful and gracious toward their sins and remember their deeds of unrighteousness no more. He further declared, **"I will be their God, and they shall be My people,"** Hebrews 8:8, 10, 12.

When the Lord went about doing good **He did great miracles.** He raised the dead, cleansed the lepers, drove out demons and healed the sick: the lame walked, the blind could see, the deaf could hear and much more, (Matt. 10:8; John 5:4-9; Luke 8:43-48; Luke 8:49-56; John 9:6-9; Luke 13:10-13; John 5:4-9; Mark 1:31, 34; Matthew 9:14-25).

He prayed for all types of sickness and all that came to Him were healed. His first miracle entailed turning water into wine for a wedding at the request of His Mother, John 2:1-11. He was also a comfort to those who mourned.

He operated in the anointing of multiplication and as He gave thanks He fed five thousand plus men (not counting the women and children) with five loaves of bread and two small fish, Matthew 14:17-21. And on another occasion, He fed four thousand men (again not counting the women and children) with seven loaves of bread and a few small fish with food left over in both cases, Matthew 15:36-37; John 6:9-14.

He walked on water and He calmed the seas, He is truly the Son of God, the Anointed One, the Messiah, Matthew 14:22-17. *Magnify the Name of Jesus, our Soon Coming King, Rev. 22:20.*

The Prophetic Scripture, the Subject and the Fulfillment

The prophetic scripture, the subject of the prophetic word and the scripture showing it was truly fulfilled just as it was prophesied, demonstrates "Every Scripture is God-breathed (given by His inspiration) and profitable for instruction, for reproof and conviction of sin, for correction of error and discipline in obedience, [and] for training in righteousness (in holy living, in conformity to God's will in thought, purpose, and action) so that the man of God may be complete and proficient, well fitted and thoroughly equipped for every good work," 2 Timothy 3:16-17.

Prophecies of the Messiah Fulfilled in Jesus Christ – Presented in their Order of Fulfillment: [4] (Scriptures are not transcribed in this resource.)

Prophetic Scripture	Subject	Fulfilled
Gen. 3:15	Seed of a woman	Gal. 4:4
Gen. 12:3	Descendant of Abraham	Matt. 1:1
Gen. 17:19	Descendant of Isaac	Luke 3:34
Num. 24:17	Descendant of Jacob	Matt. 1:2
Gen. 49:10	From the tribe of Judah	Luke 3:33
Is. 9:7	Heir to the throne of David	Luke 1:32, 33
Ps. 45:6, 7; 102:25-27	Anointed and eternal	Heb. 1:8-12
Mic. 5:2	Born in Bethlehem	Luke 2:4, 5, 7

Dan. 9:25	Time for His birth	Luke 2:1, 2
Is. 7:14	To be born of a virgin	Luke 1:26, 30, 31
Jer. 31:15	Slaughter of children	Matt. 2:16-18
Hos. 11:1	Flight to Egypt	Matt. 2:14, 15
Is. 40:3-5	The way prepared	Luke.3:3-6
Mal. 3:1	Preceded by a forerunner	Luke 7:24, 27
Mal. 4:5, 6	Preceded by Elijah	Matt. 11:13, 14
Ps. 2:7	Declared the Son of God	Matt. 3:17
Is. 9:1, 2	Galilean ministry	Matt.4:13-16
Ps. 78:2-4	Speak in parables	Matt. 13:34, 35
Deut. 18:15	A Prophet	Acts 3:20, 22
Is. 61:1	To Heal the brokenhearted	Lk. 4:18, 19
Is. 53:3	Rejected by His people, the Jews	John 1:11; Luke 23:18

Ps. 110:4	Priest after order of Melchizedek	Heb. 5:5, 6
Zech. 9:9	Triumphal entry	Mark 11:7, 9, 11
Ps. 8:2	Adored by infants	Matt. 21:15, 16
Is. 53:1	Not Believed	John 12:37, 38
Ps. 41:9	Betrayed by a close friend	Luke 22:47, 48
Zech. 11:12	Betrayed for thirty pieces of silver	Matt. 26:14, 15
Ps. 35:11	Accused by false witnesses	Mark 14:57, 58
Is. 53:7	Silent to accusations	Mark 15:4,5
Is. 50:6	Spat on and struck	Matt. 26:67
Ps. 35:19	Hated without reason	John 15:24, 25
Is. 53:5	Vicarious sacrifice	Rom. 5:6, 8
Is. 53:12	Crucified with malefactors	Mark 15:27, 28

Zech. 12:10	Pierced through hands and feet	John 20:27
Ps. 22:7, 8	Scorned and mocked	Luke 23:35
Ps. 69:9	Was reproached	Rom. 15:3
Ps. 109:4	Prayer for His enemies	Luke 23:34
Ps. 22:17, 18	Soldiers gambled for His clothing	Matt. 27:35, 36
Ps. 22:1	Forsaken by God	Matt. 27:46
Ps. 34:20	No bones broken	John 19:32, 33, 36
Zech. 12:10	His side pierced	John 19:34
Is. 53:9	Buried with the rich	Matt. 27:57-60
Ps. 16:10; 49:15	To be resurrected	Mark 16:6, 7
Ps. 68:18	His ascension to God's right hand	Mark 16:19; I Cor.15:4; Eph. 4:8

Praise to The King of kings

The following poem is by a man of God, the late, **Dr. S. M. Lockridge,** who captured and divinely expounded with great detail and revelation Who the King of kings *truly is*:

THAT'S MY KING

The Bible says my King is a seven-way king.

He's the King of the Jews; that's a racial king.

He's the King of Israel; that's a national king.

He's the King of Righteousness. He's the King of
the Ages.

He's the King of Heaven. He's the King of Glory.

He's the King of kings, and He's the Lord of lords.

That's my King

Well, I wonder do you know Him?

David said, "The Heavens declare the glory of God
and the

Firmament shows His handiwork."

My King is a sovereign King.

No means of measure can define His limitless love.

No far-seeing telescope can bring into visibility the coastline of His

shoreless supply.

No barrier can hinder Him from pouring out His blessings.

He's enduringly strong. He's entirely sincere.

He's eternally steadfast. He's immortally graceful.

He's imperially powerful. He's impartially merciful.

Do you know Him?

He's the greatest phenomenon that ever crossed the horizon of

This world. He's God's Son.

He's the sinner's Savior. He's the centerpiece of civilization.

He stands in the solitude of Himself.

He's august. He's unique. He's unparalleled. He's unprecedented.

He's the loftiest idea in literature.

He's the highest personality in philosophy.

He's the supreme problem in higher criticism.

He's the fundamental doctrine of true theology.

He's the cardinal necessity for spiritual religion.

He's the miracle of the age.

He's the superlative of everything good that you choose to call

Him. He's the only one qualified to be the all sufficient Savior.

I wonder if you know Him today.

He supplies strength for the weak. He's available for the tempted

and the tried. He sympathizes and He saves.

He strengthens and sustains. He guards and He guides.

He heals the sick. He cleanses lepers. He forgives sinners.

He discharges debtors. He delivers captives. He defends the

feeble. He blesses the young. He serves the unfortunate.

He regards the aged.

He rewards the diligent and He beautifies the meek.

I wonder if you know Him.

Well, my King is the King.

He's the key to knowledge. He's the wellspring to
wisdom.

He's the doorway of deliverance. He's the pathway
of peace.

He's the roadway of righteousness.

He's the highway of holiness. He's the gateway of
glory.

Do you know Him?

He's the master of the mighty. He's the captain of
the conquerors.

He's the head of the heroes. He's the leader of the
legislators.

He's the overseer of the over comers.

He's the governor of governors. He's the prince of
princes.

He's the King of kings and He's the Lord of lords.

That's my King.

Well, His office is manifold. His promise is sure.

His light is matchless. His goodness is limitless.

His mercy is everlasting. His love never changes.

His word is enough. His grace is sufficient.

His reign is righteousness, His yoke is easy, and his burden is light.

I wish I could describe Him to you, but He's indescribable.

He's incomprehensible. He's invincible. He's irresistible.

I'm coming to tell you, the heavens cannot contain Him,

Let alone a man explain Him.

Well, you can't get Him out of your mind.

You can't get Him off of your hand.

You can't out live Him, and you can't live without Him.

The Pharisees couldn't stand Him,

But they found out they couldn't stop Him.

Pilate couldn't find any fault in Him. The witnesses couldn't get

their testimonies to agree.

Herod couldn't kill Him.

Death couldn't handle Him, and the grave couldn't hold Him.

Yea, that's my King, that's my King.

He always has been and He always will be. He had no

predecessor and He'll have no successor. There was nobody

before Him and there'll be nobody after Him.

You can't impeach Him and He's not going to resign.

That's my King!

Father, thine is the kingdom and the power and the glory forever

and ever,

and ever, and ever, and ever. How long is that?

And ever, and ever, and when you get through with all the

forevers, then

AMEN!

APPENDIX A

A Prayer for Salvation and the Infilling of the Holy Spirit

If you are not a Born-again Christian with the Infilling (Baptism) of the Holy Spirit, or you are a Christian Believer and would like to rededicate your life to Jesus, say the following prayer. Afterwards, tell someone of the decision you have made regarding the Good News!

Dear Heavenly Father,

I come to You now, just as I am in the name of Jesus. Your Word says, "...Whosoever shall call on the name of the Lord shall be saved," Acts 2:21. And it says, "that if you confess with your mouth the Lord Jesus and believe in your heart that God raised Him from the dead, you will be saved" according to Romans 10:9.

I believe and confess now that Jesus (Yeshua) is the Son of God and He is alive today. I receive Him as my personal Lord and Savior. I ask for forgiveness and repent of my past sins and I choose to forgive others for their trespasses. Thank You Father God that Your Son has set me free from eternal darkness. I now declare that I am redeemed, I am healed, I am blessed, and I am whole. Therefore, I now have a renewed, abundant and confident life in Christ Jesus, the Messiah.

Father God, You said my Salvation would be the result of Your Holy Spirit giving me new birth by coming to live in me Romans 8:9, 11. So I ask You now for the Infilling of Your Holy Spirit as you have promised. Thank You for the gift to speak in other tongues, my spiritual prayer language that is unknown to man but known to God according to Acts 2:4 and I Corinthians 14:2. Now I bind the strong man that was sent to rob me and I plead the Blood of Jesus over my mind and mouth as I now release from my spirit my supernatural prayer language in Jesus' Mighty name. Amen! Give God Thanks!

The above Prayer is based on Romans 10:9-10 NKJV which says,

"That if you confess with your mouth the Lord Jesus and believe in your heart that God has raised Him from the dead, you will be saved. For with the heart one believes unto righteousness, and with the mouth confession is made unto salvation."

I John 2:2, 12 AMP says,

"And He [that same Jesus Himself] is the propitiation (the atoning sacrifice) for our sins, and not for ours alone but also for [the sins of] the whole world. ...*because for His name's sake your sins are forgiven [pardoned through His name and on account of confessing His name]."*

"Justified" – We are as if we never sinned! We are declared righteous, acceptable to God because of the Finished Work at the Cross where Jesus took our sins and gave us His Righteousness because in Him we have redemption through the blood! Hallelujah for a God Who Saves, Ephesians 1:7, Acts 4:12.

Salvation Scriptures:

Romans 10:9-10; John 3:14-17; John 5:24; Acts 2:21; John 10:9-18; John 6:44-51; Ps 51:5; Acts 4:12; Mt. 1:21; I Peter 1:23; Ro. 3:23; I John 1:9; Ro. 6:4; Acts 3:13-26; 2 Cor. 4:4; Eph. 2:8-10; Ro. 5:8; John 14:6; I John 4:9-10; John 3:3-6,15-16; Mt. 12:40; I Cor. 15:22; Acts 10: 40; Acts 16:31; Col. 2:6-7, Acts 15:11

Infilling of the Holy Spirit:

Acts 2:1-4; I Co. 2:4-5; Acts 10:44-48; Acts l: 5, 8; Acts 2: 39; Acts 11:16; John 4:23-24; Romans 8:6-17, 26-27; John 1:33; Eph. 6:18; Jude 1:20; I Cor. 2:14; I Cor. 6:19-20; I Cor. 14:2-15, 18; Luke 11:13; Ezekiel 11:19; I Cor. 12:7-11; Eph. 5:18; John 16:13; Gal. 5:22-23; Isaiah 11:2-3; Romans 6:1-11

APPENDIX B

What is Salvation?

God so greatly loved the world that He gave His one and only Son, that whoever believes in Him shall not perish but have eternal life, John 3:16. Because of what Jesus did on the cross, a way was made for people (Jew and Gentile) to be reconciled back to Father God through Salvation. This brought forth the "Believer," which is the One New Man, Eph. 2:14-16. "And there is salvation in *and* through no one else, *for there is no other name under heaven given among men by and in which we must be saved,"* Acts 4:12, the Amplified Bible.

In John 3:14-17 Jesus explains,

> And just as Moses lifted up the serpent in the desert [on a pole], so must [so it is necessary that] the Son of Man be lifted up [on the cross], In order that everyone who believes in Him [who cleaves to Him, trusts Him, and relies on Him] *may not perish, but* have eternal life *and* [actually] live forever! For God so greatly loved *and* dearly prized the world that He [even] gave up His only begotten (unique) Son, so that whoever believes in (trusts in, clings to,

relies on) Him shall not perish (come to destruction, be lost) but have eternal (everlasting) life. For God did not send the Son into the world in order to judge (reject, to condemn, to pass sentence on) the world, but that the world might find salvation *and* be made safe *and* sound through Him.

When you receive Yeshua HaMashiach, (Jesus the Christ, the Messiah, the Anointed One) you are saved. "For it is by free grace (God's unmerited favor) that you are saved (delivered from judgment *and* made partakers of Christ's salvation) through [your] faith. And this [salvation] is not of yourselves [of your own doing, it came not through your own striving], but it is the gift of God," Eph. 2:8.

The word "saved" is the English word for the Greek word "Sozo" which was used to define the Hebrew word "Shalom." "To be saved is defined as: to deliver or protect – heal, preserve, save, do well, be (make) whole," (Strong's Concordance).

A personal relationship with God is included. The Holy Spirit is with you, inside of you and will communicate through your spirit (heart). You are also entitled to good health, preservation, protection, provision, prosperity, favor, peace, good relationships, purpose, safety, deliverance, authority, soundness, spiritual gifts, strength, mercy, guidance, angelic help, increase, completeness and more! In other words, wholeness (Shalom).

Furthermore, the English word **"save"** is used in the New Testament to define the Hebrew word **"Shalom."** Another term used to describe "save" is **born-again.** Jesus said "unless one is born again, he cannot see the kingdom of God," John 3:1-6; I Peter 1:3.

The name Yeshua (Jesus) means Savior or Salvation. Salvation makes you whole as you grow in Messiah, Matt. 1:21. *Therefore, Yeshua restores "Shalom"* making you whole - nothing broken and nothing missing. He is the Pioneer of your Salvation, Heb. 2:10.

Jesus is also referred to as the Prince of Peace (Sar Shalom) and "Peace comes to you because you are whole!" Hebrews 13:20-21 NKJV says, "Now may the God of peace who brought up our Lord Jesus from the dead, that great Shepherd of the sheep, through the blood of the everlasting covenant, make you complete in every good work to do His will, working in you what is well pleasing in His sight, through Jesus Christ, to whom *be* glory forever and ever. Amen."

To be saved is to have Salvation (Yeshua). Everything you will ever need is found in salvation. *The most important thing about receiving salvation is in Christ you become a new creation; salvation comes with the New Covenant and salvation includes eternal life,* 2 Cor. 5:17; Jeremiah

31:31-33; Matthew 26:26-29; Luke 22:20; Romans 2:28-29; Galatians 2:16 and Galatians 3:7-14; 26-29; John 3:16, 36.

Salvation prevents anyone from perishing for their sin for eternity in outer darkness. Instead of death they will receive eternal life, John 3:36. In addition, while still on earth the Believer receives "The Blessing" which encompasses all the blessings from the Lord in the Kingdom of God.

Because we accepted the Father's sacrifice, Jesus/Yeshua, the Father *adopted us* into His Family (the Family of God, the One New Man).

Romans 8:15 says,

> For [the Spirit which] you have now received [is] not a spirit of slavery to put you once more in bondage to fear, but you have received the Spirit of adoption [the Spirit producing sonship] in [the bliss of] which we cry, Abba (Father)! Father!

The word adoption basically means a person is brought into the Family of God even though they were previously without any covenant with Him. Like all of us who are born-again (John 3:1-3) we were sinners and separated from God, but God in His mercy and grace redeemed us, purchased us and brought us into His presence. In His presence once again, this time through the blood of His only beloved Son, Jesus.

Once saved we are adopted by God, Who chose and received us as His own. What an honor, for Almighty God to choose us and then pour His love on each and every one of us. As Christian Believers in Christ Messiah, the Anointed One.

We are now eternally part of His family. His Spirit dwells in our spirit man and communes with us. Because of the adoption we become heirs of God and joint heirs with His Son, Jesus the Christ (Yeshua HaMashiach), Romans 8:17.

So how does one receive their salvation? Romans 10:9-10 NKJV says, "that if you confess with your mouth the Lord Jesus and believe in your heart that God has raised Him from the dead, you will be saved. For with the heart one believes unto righteousness, and with the mouth confession is made unto salvation."

APPENDIX C ©

Supernatural Prayer Language

I Corinthians 2:12-14 AMP says, "Now we have not received the spirit [that belongs to] the world, but **the [Holy] Spirit Who is from God, [given to us] that we might realize *and* comprehend *and* appreciate the gifts** [of divine favor and blessing so freely and lavishly] bestowed on us by God. And we are setting these truths forth in words not taught by human wisdom but taught by the [Holy] Spirit, combining *and* interpreting spiritual truths with spiritual language [to those who possess the Holy Spirit]. But the natural, nonspiritual man does not accept *or* welcome *or* admit into his heart the gifts *and* teachings *and* revelations of the Spirit of God, for they are folly (meaningless nonsense) to him; and he is incapable of knowing them [of progressively recognizing, understanding, and becoming better acquainted with them] because they are spiritually discerned *and* estimated and appreciated." It is the tongues of men and of angels, ... I Co. 13:1 NKJV.

In Romans 11:29, note "the gifts and calling of God are without repentance" and are irrevocable. **God gave to the church certain gifts to help His people while here on the earth and supernatural tongues (a language) is one of those gifts** and if it is not for today then neither are the other gifts that were given to men by the Lord for the perfecting and the full equipping of the saints that they should do the work of ministering toward building up Christ's body.

In I Corinthians 12:28 AMP it says, "God has appointed some in the church [for His own use]: first apostles (special messengers); second prophets (inspired preachers and expounders); third teachers; then wonder workers; then those with ability to heal the sick; helpers; administrators; **[speakers in] different (unknown) tongues.**"

In addition, in Ephesians 4:11 it says, "And His gifts were [varied; He Himself appointed and gave men to us] some to be apostles (special messengers), some prophets (inspired preachers and expounders), some evangelists (preachers of the Gospel, traveling missionaries), some pastors (shepherds of His flock) and teachers." These are people that are appointed by God into the fivefold ministry gifts for the perfecting of the Church, which is the Body of Christ, the One New Man in the Kingdom of God. Also, I Corinthians 12:4-11 list other gifts given by God to be used by His Saints as well.

During Jesus' ministry, He did not exercise the gift of speaking in an unknown tongue because no tongue was unknown to Him. The people did not speak in an unknown tongue either because they were not filled with the Holy Spirit at that time. However, speaking in tongues did come after Jesus died on the cross which redeemed mankind from eternal darkness and gave mankind the gift of eternal life as well as an abundant life while on earth if he or she so desired it.

He rose from the grave on the third day, and then walked the earth for forty days and on one day alone He was seen by over five hundred witnesses, I Cor. 15:6. Later He ascended into Heaven and sent back the gift of Holy Spirit, our Comforter, to be with all those who would receive Jesus (Yeshua) as their Lord and Savior.

It was not until the day of Pentecost people began speaking in an unknown tongue or language. This was the day the Jesus' church was birthed. In Acts 2:1-3 says, "And when the day of Pentecost had fully come, they were all assembled together in one place, when suddenly there came a sound from heaven like the rushing of a violent tempest blast, and it filled the whole house in which they were sitting. And there appeared to them tongues resembling fire, which were separated and distributed and which settled on each one of them." On that day in the upper room, there were one hundred and twenty men and women, the Holy Spirit rested on each one and they spoke with the gift of tongues found in I Corinthians 12:10.

The gift of tongues (my heavenly language) is proof we are filled with His Spirit to overflowing, John 14:16-17, 26; John 16:7; Acts 2:39; Acts 1:4; Luke 24:49.

Jesus told His apostles to wait for the Promise from the Father. Just as He had given them two other commandments before He left. The first was to love the Lord with all their heart, soul, mind and strength. The second was to love your neighbor as yourself. On the Day of Pentecost, Jesus' third command to them was to wait until the Promise was manifested as they and others including women received the Promise of the Father. Holy Spirit entered the upper room then entered each one of them until the Spirit overflowed each one. The proof of it was they all received the gift of tongues and spoke in other languages, even as we do today, Acts 1:4; 5:32; John 14:15-17; Eph. 5:18; Matt. 22:36-40; Mark 12:28-31.

Because they spoke in the languages of men residing in Jerusalem – Jews, devout and God-fearing men from every country under heaven who were astonished and bewildered, because each one heard them [the apostles] speaking in his own [particular] dialect and they were amazed because these people were Galileans, Acts 2:5-7.

The tongues found in I Corinthians 14:2 are **given to all today** who receive Jesus (Yeshua in Hebrew) as their Lord and Savior and have received the Infilling of the Holy Spirit to dwell inside of them, Acts 2:1-4; I Cor. 2:4-5; Acts 1:5, 8; Jn. 1:33.

Receiving the gift of Holy Spirit with the evidence of tongues is for all Believers. Acts 2:39 declares, "For the promise [of the Holy Spirit] is to *and* for you and your children, and to *and* for all that are far away, [even] to *and* for as many as the Lord our God invites *and* bids to come to Himself.

Furthermore, **the gift of tongues (I Cor. 12:10) and other gifts that are being used today** as *appointed by God will remain* until as stated in I

Corinthians 13:10, "...when the complete *and* perfect (total) comes, the incomplete and imperfect will vanish away (become antiquated, void, and superseded)."

Believers use different terms to describe they are praying in the Spirit. Some of those terms are: Praying in tongues; praying in the Spirit; praying in my heavenly language; praying in a supernatural language of the Spirit; praying in other tongues; praying in unknown tongues; praying with the Spirit and so forth.

All gifts are given by God and what God has done let no man put asunder. What He has given, whatever door He has opened, no man can shut it or change it. Therefore, as we pray and ask Him to fill us with His Holy Spirit, then rest (trust) in Him and just receive all of what He has given, created, permitted and allowed for our good.

John 4:23-24
Mark 16:16-18
Jude 1:20
Acts 1:5, 8; Acts 2:1-4, 13, 19;
Acts 2:38-39; Acts 10:38; Acts 10:44-46;
Acts 11:16; Acts 19:5-7
Romans 8:9-12; Romans 8:26-27; Romans 12:2-3
I Corinthians 14:2-5, 14, 15, 18, 22, 27, 33, 40
I Corinthians 2:14; 2 Corinthians 4:4-6
Ephesians 6:18
John 14:14-17
Luke 11:13
I John 4:1-6

Isaiah 11:2-3

The following are different ways and many reasons why Believers should speak (pray in the Spirit) in their Supernatural Prayer Language (an unknown tongue), a gift from Almighty God. Also listed are some of the reasons why many Christian Believers are hindered in this area:

1. GOD THROUGH A PERSON

A word spoken into your life from God can come through a person speaking in tongues and then prophesying to you for *edification* (upbuilding and constructive spiritual progress); *exhortation* (encouragement; warnings) and *comfort* (consolation and instructions for restoration that will bring peace and wholeness), I Corinthians 14:3.

"He who speaks in a [strange] tongue edifies *and* improves himself, but **he who prophesies [interpreting the divine will and purpose and teaching with inspiration]** edifies and improves the church *and* promotes growth [in Christian wisdom, piety, holiness, and happiness]," I Cor. 14:4.

When **God speaks through a person in an open arena** such as a church or some other meeting where people are gathered He will also give the interpretation of what has been spoken in tongues either through the person who spoke in tongues or through another person who is present. Speaking in an unknown tongue simply means you are speaking the mysteries of God. The speaker is speaking in a language that is unknown to them that involves their spirit expressing specific thoughts their mind does not understand. It is not meaningless, uncontrolled babbling as some think but a real language from the True and Living God.

In I Corinthians 12:10 the gifts of various kinds of [unknown] tongues (also seen in Acts 2:4); and the ability to interpret [such] tongues these are not entrusted to every person, but to those that are chosen by the Holy Spirit to be used for His purpose and glory. These gifts of tongues are different from the tongues in I Cor. 14:2 which are given to all Believers with the infilling of the Holy Spirit.

God will also use people's tongues (supernatural prayer language) as a weapon to fight in spiritual warfare, Revelation 2:16; Prove.18:21. The tongue located in your "mouth" which in Greek is called Stoma, means the mouth is the front or edge of a weapon.

2. A PERSON TO GOD

I Corinthians 14:2 AMP says, **"For one who speaks in an [unknown] tongue speaks not to men but to God,** for no one understands or catches his meaning, because in the [Holy] Spirit he utters secret truths and hidden things [not obvious to the understanding]."

A person is speaking directly to God without Satan or other evil forces understanding the language, therefore, these evil forces cannot hinder the answer to their prayers spoken in tongues because the person is speaking mysteries (revelation, secret truths and hidden things) not obvious to the understanding in a language that is a mixture of the tongues of men across the universe and the tongues of angels directed by the Holy Spirit. However, the Lord Almighty does understand it and it is He who shall honor the petition and answer their prayers.

When you pray in tongues you will also receive divine wisdom from God which will aid you in your everyday life. The Holy Spirit will also aid in ushering in your ministry assignment; assisting you with your business or career as well as helping you discover your purpose in life as you seek God through His Word. **The Holy Spirit will pray through you as He prays for you and others** such as love ones, neighbors, friends, leaders in the world, associates, co-workers, military personnel, strangers and those that need assistance in situations you have no knowledge of.

The Holy Spirit will pray through you via unknown tongues when you do not know "what" or "how" to pray. Romans 8: 26-27 AMP says, "So too the [Holy] Spirit comes to our aid and bears us up in our weakness; for we do not know what prayer to offer nor how to offer it worthily as we ought, but the Spirit Himself goes to meet our supplication *and* pleads in our behalf with unspeakable yearnings *and* groanings too deep for utterance. And He Who searches the hearts of men knows what is in the mind of the [Holy] Spirit [what His intent is], because the Spirit intercedes and pleads [before

God] in behalf of the saints according to *and* in harmony with God's will."

3. SINGING IN THE HOLY SPIRIT

Releases praises and thanksgiving unto God, I Corinthians 14:15 "...I will pray with my spirit [by the Holy Spirit that is within me], but I will also pray [intelligently] with my mind and understanding; **I will sing with my spirit [by the Holy Spirit that is within me],** but I will sing [intelligently] with my mind and understanding also."

Many times, as we are led by the Holy Spirit to sing in tongues and give praises it is because our prayers have been heard and a release to pray about a given thing or person has been accomplished and it is also possible the answer has already been sent. The Holy Spirit will sometimes show you who or what you are praying for or about. The Holy Spirit through your tongues will pray a perfect prayer and issue all that is needed to accomplish an assignment.

4. BUILDING YOURSELF UP IN THE HOLY FAITH

In the Book of Jude 1:20 AMP it says, "But you, beloved, build yourselves up [founded] on your most holy faith [make progress, rise like an edifice higher and higher], praying in the Holy Spirit."

As you pray in the Holy Spirit it will help you to produce and maintain the fruit of the Spirit found in Galatians 5:22-23 (love, joy, peace, patience, gentleness, goodness, faithfulness, kindness and self-control). Thereby helping you to live and maintain holiness because you have been strengthened in areas where you were weak or had challenges.

Praying in the Spirit and understanding along with studying the Word of God in the areas where you have weaknesses, challenges or sin can be turned around and deliverance can come forth and stay as you remain built-up in His Word and in the Spirit.

In addition, as you pray in tongues spiritual gifts can be released into your life that may be lying dormant inside of you, spiritual gifts such as the gift of faith, the gift of healing, the gift of miracles, the gift of discernment and so on as listed in I Corinthians 12:4-11.

TONGUES – A SUPERNATURAL SPIRITUAL PRAYER LANGUAGE AND REASONS TO USE IT

When I Pray in the Spirit, Praying from My Heart in an Unknown Spiritual Language or Tongue:

I am being enlightened and empowered with divine wisdom, ability, strength, instructions, directions, and revelation. Holy Spirit prays through my spiritual language and will pray what is needed and to fulfill the call of God on my life.

The manifestation that came when I received Holy Spirit was the gift of an unknown tongue (language). When I speak in tongues my prayers, requests I speak goes directly into the throne room of God, I Cor. 14:2.

The Word also says, I "should pray [for the power] to interpret what I say," and this should also apply if one is praying in their spiritual language in an open arena with other people present, I Corinthians 14:4, 13.

I am filling the atmosphere around me with God's presence and glory.

I am praying the mind of God; praying the wonderful strategies, works and thoughts of God.

I am praying the will of God, those things that have been freely given by God to me and other Believers.

I am praying directly to God, I Corinthians 14:2, 16. I receive the Gift the Father sent because Jesus made a way for His church to receive the Gift of Holy Spirit, I Cor. 12:31. Because of Jesus our spirit comes alive when we receive salvation and are saved as Holy Spirit comes to dwell in us. Then Holy Spirit gives our spiritual language to us when we ask. Now we can communicate with our Heavenly Father Spirit to spirit.

The Holy Spirit is a special Gift from Father God, Luke 24:49; Acts 1:4 John 14:16, 17, 26; John 16:7, 13; John 15:26; Acts 1:5; Acts 2:38; Acts10:45; Eph. 1:13.

When I allow my spirit man to pray for me I enter into the rest of God. This is especially helpful if there is a crisis or some sort of trauma has taken place. Praying in the spirit will help to sustain me in a crisis.

Praying in an unknown tongue (my supernatural prayer language) will activate the fruit of the Spirit and spiritual gifts God has for me, Gal. 5:22-23 and I Cor. 12:7-11.

As I pray in tongues it crucifies the flesh and humbles the pride of man which protects me. Because pride comes before the fall, I Pet. 5:6; Ro. 5:10; Prov. 16:18.

I am speaking mysteries – secret truths that can only be known by revelation and receiving understanding, I Corinthians 14:2; (Secrets and mysteries are God's will, His plans and purposes).

I am building myself up in my spirit man. The Bible says He who speaks in a tongue edifies himself, I Cor. 14:4. This would include building up your soul (mind, will and emotions) and your body especially your immune system.

I am also building myself up [founded] on my most holy faith [making progress, rise like an edifice higher and higher]. I am ministering to myself when I am praying in the Spirit, Jude 1:20 AMP.

I am led by the Holy Spirit to pray when I do not know what to pray, how to pray effectively for a certain matter or situation or my mind is too tired to concentrate on prayer.

I am producing unity in the Kingdom of God. Children of God are speaking in unity when they pray in tongues. God's people should live together in unity, Ps. 133:1; Eph. 4:3; Acts 2:1; John 17:20-23.

I am quenching the fiery darts of the wicked with a watery shield. Your shield (Eph. 6:16) is living water, which is the Holy Spirit that flows out of your belly according to John 7:38

I am alert and watch with strong purpose and perseverance, interceding on behalf of all the Saints (God's consecrated people), Ephesians 6:18 AMP

I shall receive power (ability, efficiency, and might) when the Holy Spirit has come upon me. Tongues are the evidence of power within me, Acts 1:8

I am operating in a gift proven to reach the true peace of God. It will also help to maintain it. No one can tame the tongue, the most powerful member in the human body, except the Holy Spirit, James 3:8. Praying in tongues will enable you to have better control of your mouth because God can tame the tongue as you speak in your spiritual language. Death and life are in the power of the tongue, Prov. 18:21. Our tongue is connected to our spirit, therefore, as the spirit in you is maturing and built up from praying in tongues, it will enable you to have more control over your mouth. I can also ask Holy Spirit to set a guard over my mouth as I speak in the understanding (my everyday language), Psalm 141:3.

I am releasing spiritual gifts that may be lying dormant inside of me, spiritual gifts such as the gift of faith, healing, miracles, prophecy, and so on, I Co. 12:4-11.

I am releasing praises and thanksgiving unto God as I sing in the spirit, I Co 14:15.

I am praying in a language Satan cannot understand and doing warfare against the powers of darkness, Mark 16:17.

I am receiving a supernatural refreshment as well as entering into a supernatural rest

I am praying and prophesying my future as the Holy Spirit is praying for me establishing things in my life, in the spiritual kingdom first, and at the appointed time they shall manifest in the natural

I am praying "with my spirit [by the Holy Spirit that is within me], but I will also pray [intelligently] with my mind *and* understanding;" ...Because of the Holy Spirit my mind is alert and keen, I Corinthians 14:15 AMP.

The Spirit gives life and praying in your spiritual prayer language can also cause you to look younger than your age; it helps to build a spiritual foundation in your life.

When you pray in tongues it does not come from the speech center in your brain like it does when you speak or sing in the understanding (your regular language), I Cor. 14:14. While praying in the Spirit your mind is still conscious and aware but unfruitful because it is not supplying nor understanding the words spoken. While praying in the understanding, your voice is an expression of the thoughts in your mind.

Quickest avenue to the supernatural: gives divine encouragement, power comes, and boldness comes at its highest degree, it also releases a divine expectation and experiences in the spirit you cannot get any other way. Furthermore, tongues increase our ability to walk in the Spirit, be led by the Spirit, develop the fruit of the Spirit and manifest the gifts of the Spirit among other spiritual benefits that Jesus left for us to have. He gave us the spiritual blessings.

I am releasing spiritual truth and making it more real so I am bold and not afraid of problems.

I am cutting a new path in the supernatural which affects everything around you, I am invading the supernatural

I am removing blind spots in the spiritual realm because God opens blinded eyes and creating a new ability to yield in order for God to place me on another level.

I am birthing things in the spirit realm that have no other way to come into existence.

I am obtaining hidden wisdom by going into a certain realm of divinity.

HINDRANCES AND BLOCKS TO SPEAKING IN AN UNKNOWN TONGUE

*Why are so many people in **fear** about speaking in an unknown tongue (a language that is unknown to them but known to God)?*

First of all, **let us clarify "fear" is not from God.** Second Timothy 1:7 KJV, states, "For God hath not given us the spirit of fear; but of power, and of love, and of a sound mind;" – (a calm *and* well-balanced mind and discipline *and* self-control," AMP).

Satan the adversary brings the fear, concerns and worries to prevent others from enjoying a gift from our true and only God. A gift that will give them great benefits and work against the kingdom of darkness which the adversary does not want and greatly opposes.

To some unknown tongues is seen as a mysterious and frightening thing and they are afraid they will lose control of when and where they speak. I Cor. 14:32 AMP, says "… (the speakers in tongues) are under the speaker's control." In reality, you can start and stop speaking in an unknown language just like any other language. For example, if your first language is English and you know French, Spanish, Hebrew, Swahili, Chinese or some other language, you can stop speaking in English and speak in one of the other languages at your will and stop when you desire.

It is the same thing for the unknown tongue because it is a "language." A language you have no one understands but God! He can give you the interpretation or revelation about what is being said but the purpose is to have a language the adversary does not understand. Keep in mind, however, there is a gift of Divers Kinds of Tongues (I Cor. 12:10) in which the speaker is speaking in a language unknown to them but known to other people listening that may be from another country that God chooses to direct a word to them in their language (Acts 2:4-7). Another example is we all have the ability to sing and we can sing when we choose to and we can stop when we choose to because we are in control.

Some fear they will lose control of their mind or body. When some people first receive the Infilling of the Holy Spirit they are emotional or excited and when they receive it they may speak a long time or some may even fall under the power of God. On the other hand, some may receive and not speak right away; or some may receive and speak and are full of joy; some may speak and thank God and go on with their day. Each experience is an individual one and no same set of emotions will be reflected in everyone when they first receive their prayer language. Some individuals are more emotional than others. Emotions are from God and there isn't anything wrong with showing them and showing one's appreciation for what He has given them.

Some are in fear they are speaking a language that is of the devil even though the Bible has made it clear it is the will of God and it is from Him, (Acts 2:5-7; I Cor.14; Eph. 6:18; Mark 16:17, and so on). At best the adversary will try to counterfeit tongues but unsuccessfully because the Holy Spirit knows how to protect His own and expose a plan of deception. In Luke 11:11-13 the Lord did not say asking for or receiving His gifts would be dangerous. He assures us if we ask God for His good gifts, the Heavenly Father would give the Holy Spirit to those who ask and not allow us to receive evil or something that would be harmful.

Some are taught against speaking in unknown tongues in their churches and seminaries out of ignorance. Their instructors not knowing the validity of this gift or the will of God who sent His Spirit even though Holy Spirit kept giving them clear *and* loud expression [in each tongue in appropriate words], Acts 2:4 AMP. But by refusing the Holy Spirit and allowing Him to move at will, the result was they passed down erroneous information to their congregations and to seminary students.

Some assume they are not speaking in a "real language" so why do it? The truth is it is a very real language that is of angels and of men directed by the Holy Spirit (I Cor. 13:1; Acts 19:6) and is simply a language unknown to the "speaker." Furthermore, negative thoughts or false accusations are sent to you through others Satan can use to tell you that you do not have it. Take that as confirmation you do have it because the adversary would not bother if you really did not have it! Further confirmation you are praying in the Holy Spirit, your unknown tongue, is you will begin to yield fruit in your life. You will begin to see supernatural results because the Holy Spirit will pray for things to connect and open doors you have no knowledge of. You will see positive changes taking place when you are faithful to communicate with the Lord daily. You will be more sensitive to the Spirit of God and more yielded to follow His leading.

Some people don't want to face persecution (being separated out or mocked by others) so even if they did pray in the Spirit they would be very cautious of where they prayed and who knew about it. One must make up their mind if they are here to please man or to please God. Some persecution comes with being a Believer but the Word says, when they despise you, persecute you or exclude you, you are to rejoice because it confirms your reward is rich and great and you are a blessed person, Luke 6:22-23.

What if you strongly desire to speak in your supernatural prayer language **but somehow just cannot seem to release it** because of fear or prior false teaching on the subject? There are a number of things you can do:

- **You can pray and ask God to release the gift to you.** If you know you have fear you can ask for forgiveness for allowing the fear to stop you and by faith receive the "Promise" which is His Holy Spirit.
- You can have others stand in agreement and pray with you and/or anoint you with oil and lay hands on you as they pray for you and you ask God to release the gift of tongues to you

then wait on God and don't give up if it does not happen immediately.

- If you still have not received your mind may be in the way refusing to yield control of your voice to your spirit. You can plead the blood of Jesus over your mind and mouth and command the release of your spiritual language that has been promised to you.

- You can help by speaking forth whatever comes out of your mouth regardless of how it sounds. The release of tongues (your spiritual language) is a very natural thing according to the Word of God. You can help by starting to praise God and let it flow from there by choosing to simply stop speaking in the understanding (words your mind can understand). Now let sounds come from your spirit, random sounds come out of your mouth as you praise and express your love for Him. This will break the control your mind has over your vocal cords. The first few sounds will probably not be your prayer language but sounds that come out because you are refusing to allow your mind to provide the words so your spirit can take over and speak and flow over time.

- You can start by speaking softly to yourself so the sounds you make won't distract you as you continue to honor God by speaking in a language you can communicate and draw closer to Him with.

- Just remember it is a new language to you and just like a baby begins to speak a few words in the beginning over time as they continue speaking it will develop into a beautiful language.

- **Any Spirit-filled Christian Believer has the gift to speak in tongues from God.** Once you are Born-again (received Salvation) you then ask and receive the infilling of the Holy Spirit and believe God is faithful to give it to you when you ask, Mark 11:24. You may speak anytime; it is a gift to you to give you power, peace and other benefits in this earth realm.

- **Pray in the Spirit on every occasion** (Eph. 6:18): morning, during the day, evening, while driving, playing, doing work whenever you feel an unction to do so, or if someone has a prayer request or you sense someone needs prayer or the Holy Spirits places someone or something on your heart or mind. You can pray softly and be just as effective because the Spirit of God is seeing and hearing your heart not just the sounds that are coming from your mouth.

NOTES

Chapter One:
The Name that is Above Every Name

1. Messianic Rabbi Zev Porat, Guest Lynn Leahz program, 2017 Answering Questions regarding use of the Name of God and the Jewish People. www.messiahofisraelministries.org

Chapter Two:
The Person Jesus

1. H. A. Maxwell Whyte, *The Power of the Blood.* New Kensington: Whitaker House, 1973
2. ibid
3. ibid
4. The New Unger's Bible Dictionary. Chicago: Moody press, 1988
5. ibid
6. Eitan Bar, *Is Jesus Really From the Line of David,* article, 2017. He serves One for Israel Ministry in Israel as the Director of Media & Evangelism as well as the Producer of *I Met Messiah* and the Producer of *Answering Rabbinic Objections to Jesus.*
7. ibid
8. ibid
9. ibid
10. ibid

Chapter Three:
The Commission Sent from Heaven

1. Zola Levitt, *Levitt letter page 32*: Dallas: Levitt.com, 2018 Zola Levitt Ministries
2. Joseph Prince, *Destined To Reign, Devotional.* Tulsa: Harrison House, 2008
3. ibid

Chapter Four:
The Gift, His Anointing Abides in You

1. Joyce Meyer, *Hearing from God Each Morning.* New York: Faith Words, 2010

Chapter Six:
His Kingdom, Kingship and Royal Power

1. Disciple's Study Bible, NIV Footnote. Nashville: Holman Bible Publishers, 1988
2. ibid

Chapter Seven:
The King of kings and You

1. Disciple's Study Bible, NIV Footnote. Nashville: Holman Bible Publishers, 1988
2. Joseph Prince, *Destined To Reign, Devotional.* Tulsa: Harrison House, 2008
3. ibid

4. Ever Increasing Faith Study Bible, NKJV. Los Angeles: Faith One Publishing, 1994 and Nashville: Thomas Nelson Publishers, 1982

About the Author

Audrey L. Dickey, D.Min., Ph.D. is an apostle, prophetic voice, author and conference speaker. She ministers the Word and counsels prophetically to advance the fivefold ministry in the Kingdom of God. Her books include spiritual warfare strategies and tools for marriages, families, finances, everyday life experiences and Kingdom business. Since her youth she has seen signs and wonders, healings and prophecies come to pass through the power of God. Dr. Audrey holds a Doctor of Philosophy in Religious Studies and a Doctor of Ministry with emphasis in Biblical Counseling from FICU in California. She is also a member of the American Association of Christian Counselors (AACC). She along with her husband, Robert L. Dickey, Ph.D. received a vision to establish an international apostolic, prophetic ministry. They are the founders and CEO's of Christian Love Glory International Center as well as the founders and apostles of Christian Love Fellowship Church, Inc. This Fivefold multi-cultural ministry includes covenant restoration of the One New Man and will oversee designated marketplace businesses. Drs. Robert and Audrey Dickey have five children and make their home in Los Angeles, California.

To Contact the Author:
Dr. Audrey L. Dickey
P. O. 48288
Los Angeles, CA 90048
www.robertandaudreydickeyministries.org

Other Books by Audrey L. Dickey

<u>GOD'S WAY SERIES</u>

God's Way and Marriage

God's Way and Family

God's Way and the Blended Family

God's Way and Finances

God's Way and Divorce

God's Way and Spiritual Warfare